D0392061

DATE DUE

AUG 0 3 2009		

North & South Korea

Other Books of Related Interest:

"Congress shall make
no law ... abridging
the freedom of speech,
or of the press."

First Amendment to the U.S. Constitution

The basic foundation of our democracy is the First Amendment guarantee of freedom of expression. The Opposing Viewpoints series is dedicated to the concept of this basic freedom
and the idea that it is more important to practice it than to
enshrine it.

OPPOSING
VIEWPOINTS®
SERIES

North & South Korea

Louise I. Gerdes, Book Editor

GREENHAVEN PRESS
An imprint of Thomson Gale, a part of The Thomson Corporation

THOMSON
———＊———™
GALE

Detroit • New York • San Francisco • New Haven, Conn. • Waterville, Maine • London

THOMSON

＊™

GALE

Christine Nasso, *Publisher*
Elizabeth Des Chenes, *Managing Editor*

© 2007 The Gale Group.

Star logo is a trademark and Gale and Greenhaven Press are registered trademarks used herein under license.

For more information, contact:
Greenhaven Press
27500 Drake Rd.
Farmington Hills, MI 48331-3535
Or you can visit our Internet site at http://www.gale.com

Cover photograph reproduced by permission of photos.com.

ISBN-13: 978-0-7377-3765-3 (hardcover)
ISBN-10: 0-7377-3765-4 (hardcover)
ISBN-13: 978-0-7377-3766-0 (pbk.)
ISBN-10: 0-7377-3766-2 (pbk.)

Library of Congress Control Number: 2007932107

Table of Contents

Chapter 3: What Policies Will Best Serve South Korea?

Why Consider Opposing Viewpoints?

> *"The only way in which a human being can make some approach to knowing the whole of a subject is by hearing what can be said about it by persons of every variety of opinion and studying all modes in which it can be looked at by every character of mind. No wise man ever acquired his wisdom in any mode but this."*
>
> John Stuart Mill

In our media-intensive culture it is not difficult to find differing opinions. Thousands of newspapers and magazines and dozens of radio and television talk shows resound with differing points of view. The difficulty lies in deciding which opinion to agree with and which "experts" seem the most credible. The more inundated we become with differing opinions and claims, the more essential it is to hone critical reading and thinking skills to evaluate these ideas. Opposing Viewpoints books address this problem directly by presenting stimulating debates that can be used to enhance and teach these skills. The varied opinions contained in each book examine many different aspects of a single issue. While examining these conveniently edited opposing views, readers can develop critical thinking skills such as the ability to compare and contrast authors' credibility, facts, argumentation styles, use of persuasive techniques, and other stylistic tools. In short, the Opposing Viewpoints series is an ideal way to attain the higher-level thinking and reading skills so essential in a culture of diverse and contradictory opinions.

In addition to providing a tool for critical thinking, Opposing Viewpoints books challenge readers to question their own strongly held opinions and assumptions. Most people form their opinions on the basis of upbringing, peer pressure, and personal, cultural, or professional bias. By reading carefully balanced opposing views, readers must directly confront new ideas as well as the opinions of those with whom they disagree. This is not to simplistically argue that everyone who reads opposing views will—or should—change his or her opinion. Instead, the series enhances readers' understanding of their own views by encouraging confrontation with opposing ideas. Careful examination of others' views can lead to the readers' understanding of the logical inconsistencies in their own opinions, perspective on why they hold an opinion, and the consideration of the possibility that their opinion requires further evaluation.

Evaluating Other Opinions

To ensure that this type of examination occurs, Opposing Viewpoints books present all types of opinions. Prominent spokespeople on different sides of each issue as well as well-known professionals from many disciplines challenge the reader. An additional goal of the series is to provide a forum for other, less-known, or even unpopular viewpoints. The opinion of an ordinary person who has had to make the decision to cut off life support from a terminally ill relative, for example, may be just as valuable and provide just as much insight as a medical ethicist's professional opinion. The editors have two additional purposes in including these less-known views. One, the editors encourage readers to respect others' opinions—even when not enhanced by professional credibility. It is only by reading or listening to and objectively evaluating others' ideas that one can determine whether they are worthy of consideration. Two, the inclusion of such viewpoints encourages the important critical thinking skill of objectively evaluating an author's credentials and bias. This evaluation will illuminate an author's reasons for taking a particular stance on an issue and will aid in readers' evaluation of the author's ideas.

It is our hope that these books will give readers a deeper understanding of the issues debated and an appreciation of the complexity of even seemingly simple issues when good and honest people disagree. This awareness is particularly important in a democratic society such as ours in which people enter into public debate to determine the common good. Those with whom one disagrees should not be regarded as enemies but rather as people whose views deserve careful examination and may shed light on one's own.

Thomas Jefferson once said that "difference of opinion leads to inquiry, and inquiry to truth." Jefferson, a broadly educated man, argued that "if a nation expects to be ignorant and free . . . it expects what never was and never will be." As individuals and as a nation, it is imperative that we consider the opinions of others and examine them with skill and discernment. The Opposing Viewpoints series is intended to help readers achieve this goal.

David L. Bender and Bruno Leone,
Founders

Introduction

> "*Korea has a history of fierce regional rivalries and North/South fissures that predate 1945. But even stronger is the ethnic identity that burns furiously on both sides of the demilitarized zone.*"
>
> —Philip Bowring,
> political commentator

A nighttime satellite image of the Korean peninsula reveals a South Korea brightly lit like its neighbors Japan and China. In North Korea, however, light is conspicuously absent. Although an estimated 22 million people populate North Korea, their presence in the photo is imperceptible. "Except for the lights of Pyongyang [the capital], North Korea looks little different today than 5,000 years ago, as if the country has never discovered electricity," writes journalist Joshua Zumbrun. Life in North Korea is indeed dramatically different from life in South Korea.

Today's divided Korea has its roots in Cold War tensions between the United States and the Soviet Union. In the closing days of World War II, troops from both nations, then allies, entered Korea and liberated its people from Japanese occupation. The Soviet Union occupied Korea north of the 38th parallel and the United States occupied the territory to the south. A 1947 United Nations resolution called for the election of a united Korean government, but relations between the Soviet Union and the United States had chilled, and the Soviet Union refused to approve the plan. Elections were, however, held in the South, and Syngman Rhee was elected as the first leader of the Republic of Korea (South Korea).

While elections were being held in the South, the Soviet Union established a Communist government—the Democratic People's Republic of Korea—in the north. Kim Il Sung, who had helped lead the Korean resistance to Japanese occupation, became the nation's first leader in 1949. Kim vowed to reunite the Koreas under his rule, and after building a large army, invaded the South. With the help of superior Soviet weapons and training, North Korean forces overwhelmed South Korea. In response, United Nations and South Korean forces led by U.S. General Douglas MacArthur drove out the invaders and almost took the entire peninsula before Communist China, North Korea's northern neighbor, sent its own forces to support North Korea. The war continued for three years, devastating the Korean peninsula: Millions of Koreans died, the land was scarred by heavy bombing, and industry and agriculture were nearly wiped out. An armistice ended the fighting and established a cease-fire line near the 38th parallel. Negotiations for a peace treaty between North and South Korea, however, failed to materialize, and only a suspension of hostilities remains.

In the eyes of many, the militaristic society that evolved in North Korea is a product of the U.S. presence in the South. Following the war, the United States bolstered South Korea's military with U.S. ground troops, backed by U.S. naval forces in the Pacific and the U.S. nuclear deterrent. As a result, Kim and his son and successor, Kim Jong Il, have focused most of the nation's energies on creating a militarized society with a well-quipped million-man army. Relations between North Korea and the United States are shaped by North Korea's attempt to increase its military strength by developing nuclear weapons and U.S. efforts to thwart these efforts. Mutual threats and concessions have been the norm between the United States and North Korea for decades. Tensions escalated when the administration of President George W. Bush took a harder line against North Korea, calling it part of an "axis of evil" that included Iran and Iraq. This tension reached a peak on October

9, 2006, when North Korea announced that it had tested a nuclear weapon. Efforts to resolve this crisis continued into 2007.

Political developments in North Korea have also contributed to the North and South Korean divide. North Korea is an isolated nation run by a paternalistic, authoritarian regime. Although Kim Il Sung was a more popular leader with his people than those in the South, who many believed to be mere puppets of the American occupation, political dissent was and continues to be harshly punished. Claims of human rights abuses are widespread. Kim established a unique brand of communism guided by the principle of *juché*, self-reliance, which kept foreigners at arm's length. While the Soviet Union maintained forces in its Eastern European satellites, it withdrew forces from Korea in 1948, leaving Kim to develop his own government. Kim's communism was influenced by Korean social values. Traditional Communist principles allowed Kim to break down old political hierarchies, but Confucian social values enabled him to create a "new hierarchical structure even more rigid than the old, and just as resistant to change," writes Korean scholar Charles K. Armstrong. Kim's focus on independence and self-reliance, however, isolated the nation. When the Soviet Union dissolved in the late 1980s, North Korea became further isolated, having lost its primary source of external support. The economy suffered, leading to nationwide poverty and starvation.

While North Korea isolated itself, South Korea expanded its connections with the rest of the world, ultimately becoming the world's eleventh largest economy. With the help of foreign aid and the security of U.S. military support, South Korea focused on modernizing and developing its economy. Democracy, however, was slow in coming to South Korea. During the three decades following the war, South Korea was led by corrupt, authoritarian leaders who, like Kim, suppressed political dissent. Some blame the United States for supporting these regimes, putting anticommunism ahead of political freedom. In the 1980s, however, mass protests led to more open elections, and the first civilian president, Kim Young Sam, was elected in 1992.

The first South Korean leader to reach out to North Korea was Kim Dae Jung, a dissident in South Korea's early years, who was elected in 1998. Despite their differences, the dream of reunification remains alive for many Koreans. Indeed, many in South Korea no longer see North Korea as an enemy. "Their blood brothers in the North," writes former ambassador to South Korea, James Lilley, "are failing economically, starving, and suffering. Yet they remain proud and defiant demanding respect, dignity, and sovereignty—very Korean traits." For the first time since the Korean War, in June 2000 Kim Jong Il and Kim Dae Jung met in Pyongyang. This meeting, one step in a policy of engagement with North Korea known as the "sunshine policy," aggravated the growing rift between South Korea and the United States, who had hoped South Korea would take a harder line against North Korea.

While South Korean efforts to engage North Korea have met with substantial resistance, the Korean people share a common bond that some argue will bring an end to the divide and bring light once again to North Korea. The authors in this volume explore these and other issues concerning the Koreas in the following chapters of Opposing Viewpoints: *North & South Korea*: Does North Korea Pose a Serious Threat? What Policies Toward North Korea Are Best? What Policies Will Best Serve South Korea? and Democracy and Human Rights in North and South Korea.

OPPOSING
VIEWPOINTS®
SERIES

CHAPTER 1

Does North Korea Pose a Serious Threat?

Chapter Preface

O n October 9, 2006, North Korea announced that it had tested a nuclear weapon. The international community quickly condemned the action. The United States claimed the test was a "provocative act." China denounced the act as "brazen." Japan said the test was "unpardonable" and feared the region was "entering a new, dangerous nuclear age." Almost as quickly analysts began to debate the significance of the threat posed by North Korea. One question that reflects this debate is whether North Korea's nuclear test might encourage other nations, particularly Iran, to do the same. While some commentators claim that North Korea's nuclear test might indeed encourage Iran to develop its own nuclear weapons, others assert that any links between these two nations are exaggerated.

Some observers assert that unless the United States changes its policies in the Middle East, Iran will follow North Korea's lead and develop its own nuclear weapons. These analysts allege that the Iranian government views North Korea's nuclear test as a response to U.S. economic and diplomatic pressure. Similar pressure on Iran, they argue, will have the same result. Indeed, reports from within Iran support this claim. "North Korea's nuclear test was a reaction to America's threats and humiliation," reports Iran's state-run radio. "Such pressure finally led North Korea to conduct its nuclear test." Some observers therefore caution policy makers that the U.S. presence in neighboring Afghanistan and Iraq poses a national security threat to Iran. "It all boils down to questions of national security," claims former negotiator Kaveh Afrasiabi. Saeed Laylaz, a security analyst in Tehran, agrees that American actions will determine Iran's strategic choices. "Because the [Iranian] regime is convinced that the US wants to [change the regime], they believe they have a temporary opportunity to protect themselves [using] a nuclear program as a shield," he asserts.

Other analysts dispute this claim, arguing that the choices facing Iran and North Korea are unique. Foreign relations expert Michael A. Levi contends that Iran "does not have to follow the North Korean route to enhance its security." He claims, for example, that developing nuclear weapons would not offer Iran the protection enjoyed by North Korea. The U.S. decision not to attack North Korea is based on factors other than mere deterrence. North Korea's million-man army and its conventional capability could destroy much of Seoul, South Korea's capital. Moreover, South Korea and China are strongly opposed to such an attack. "Iran's situation is different," Levi argues. "Its neighbors are far less interested in protecting it, and its ability to wreak havoc in Iraq and Israel, while substantial, is less imposing than North Korea's ability to devastate Seoul," he asserts. Nevertheless, although like-minded analysts believe that North Korea and Iran are isolated cases, they do argue, however, that the U.S. response to North Korea must be fashioned with Iran in mind. If Iran is skeptical of American diplomatic efforts regarding North Korea, "it will doubt the sincerity of American offers to talk with Iranian diplomats," Levi maintains.

Whether Iran will follow North Korea's lead and develop and test nuclear weapons remains a controversial question. The authors of the viewpoints in the following chapter debate other issues in answer to the question: Does North Korea pose a serious threat?

> "[North Korea's nuclear] test, the culmi-
> nation of six years of failed diplomacy
> ... poses a serious threat to the United
> States and to our allies."

North Korea Poses a Serious Nuclear Threat

William Perry

North Korea has proven nuclear capability and poses a serious threat to international peace, claims William Perry in the follow-ing viewpoint. If the United States and nations such as China and South Korea do not prevent North Korea from moving for-ward with its nuclear program, North Korea might further in-crease its nuclear arsenal, he maintains. Moreover, Perry argues, North Korea could also sell nuclear bombs or plutonium to other nations. Coercive threats may be the only way to contain North Korea's nuclear program, he asserts. Perry, a former secretary of defense, is a fellow at the conservative Hoover Institution.

As you read, consider the following questions:

1. According to Perry, how long has North Korea been working to achieve a nuclear weapon program?
2. What was the essence of the September 2005 under-standing in the six-party talks, in the author's view?

William Perry, "North Korea," *statement before the Committee on House Foreign Af-fairs*, January 18, 2007.

3. In the author's opinion, what would be the most feasible form of coercion to be used in negotiating with North Korea?

In September of last year [2006], the North Koreans conducted a test of an atomic bomb. This test, the culmination of six years of failed diplomacy with North Korea, poses a serious threat to the United States and to our allies in the region. My testimony today will discuss the North Korean nuclear program by asking three related questions:

- Why should we care?

- How did they get there?

- What should we do about it?

We should not care because North Korea is going to put its bombs in missile warheads and fire them at us. They are still far from having that capability, and even if they get it, deterrence would still be effective. The North Korean regime is not seeking to commit suicide.

We should care because a North Korean nuclear program can stimulate a nuclear arms race in the Pacific, with a host of dangerous consequences. We should care because if North Korea proceeds unchecked, there will be very little chance of stopping Iran. And we should care because a Korean or Iranian bomb could end up in the hands of a terror group who in turn could detonate it in one of our cities.

North Korea has been working to achieve a nuclear weapon program for more than twenty years. And the United States has been working that same period of time to contain or delay that program. . . .

Misunderstanding the Understanding

There have been five meetings in Beijing, [China] the last four involving six parties (United States, North Korea, China, Russia, Japan, and South Korea). The first three meetings in

Beijing, all in the first term of the [George W.] Bush administration, made no apparent progress. The fourth meeting, held in September 2005 by our new negotiator, Ambassador Chris Hill, resulted in an understanding.

The essence of the understanding was: North Korea said that they were prepared to give up their nuclear weapons; the United States said that it was prepared to pledge not to initiate military force to overthrow the North Korean regime; and all sides agreed that North Korea was entitled to have a peaceful nuclear program. But the day after the meeting concluded, there were conflicting reports from Pyongyang, [North Korea's capital] and Washington as to what the third component of the understanding really said. Washington said that full disarmament had to be the first step; only then would they "consider" North Korea's request for a light-water reactor. Pyongyang says that the light-water reactor must be agreed to before any disarmament begins. Thus there was a fundamental misunderstanding about the "understanding."

In the meantime, the North Korean nuclear program moved ahead at full speed. Unlike the faulty intelligence information the United States had on Iraq before the Iraq War, we had substantial and solid information about North Korea's plutonium-based weapon program. My assessment of their status as of . . . June [2006] was as follows:

It was certain that they had the fuel for making about 8 nuclear bombs;

It was highly probable that this fuel had been reprocessed to make plutonium;

It was highly probable that the resulting plutonium had already been used to make some or all of the bombs;

It was likely that North Korea would conduct tests with some of these bombs; and

It was certain that North Korea had restarted their research reactor at Yongbyon to produce more plutonium.

We had much less confidence in information about their uranium-based weapon program: American government officials have said that North Korea has a covert weapons program based on highly-enriched uranium. North Korea says they do not. A Pakistani scientist says that he gave technology and materials to North Korea for a highly-enriched uranium program. Libya reports that they have bought material and equipment for a highly-enriched uranium program from North Korea. A reasonable conclusion was that North Korea did have a highly-enriched uranium program, but that it was probably not close to production.

A Nuclear North Korea

In sum, the evidence in June [2006] was strong that North Korea was well embarked in building a sizable nuclear arsenal. Given this background, the report in late June that North Korea was preparing to test an ICBM [Intercontinental Ballistic Missile] was particularly ominous. Dr. [Ashton] Carter and I were sufficiently concerned that we wrote an op-ed piece for the *Washington Post*. Our op-ed recommended that the United States take a very hard line with the North Koreans, telling them to take the ICBM off the launch pad and return it to their storage area or the United States would destroy it. Of course, we did not really want to have to carry out such an attack. We hoped that the op-ed would cause the parties involved to realize how serious the situation had become. That it would stimulate China to get serious about real pressure on North Korea; that it would stimulate North Korea to stop playing at brinksmanship; and that it would stimulate the United States to get serious about negotiating with North Korea. Instead the administration responded to the North Korean preparations with a press statement that they would consider the launch of an ICBM as "unacceptable." North Korea launched the ICBM. To add insult to injury, they launched it on the 4th of July, and added to their fireworks display the launch of 4 medium-range missiles. The administration then released another press statement deploring the action. . . .

Late in September [2006] we saw activity underway in North Korea indicating that a nuclear test was in preparation. The administration again warned that such a test would be unacceptable. The Chinese government sent an envoy to North Korea to urge them not to conduct the test. The United Nations released a resolution demanding that North Korea not conduct the test.

On 6 October [2006], North Korea conducted a nuclear bomb test. It was low yield, so it is reasonable to conclude that it was not a complete success, but it was a nuclear bomb, fueled by plutonium. On the basis of that test and certain other information, I revised my estimate of North Korea's nuclear capability. My October [2006] estimate is similar to the estimate I made in June, except that the word "likely" is replaced by the word "certain." Shortly after the nuclear test I wrote another op-ed for the *Washington Post*. I pointed out that because of past inactions on the part of the United States and the international community, there were no attractive options left for stopping North Korea from having a meaningful nuclear capability.

In sum, I believe that we are in a very deep hole today with North Korea. So how should we proceed—is there a way we can dig out of that hole? Of course we would like North Korea to roll back their entire program, but it will be very hard to get North Korea to give up a capability they already have. But we should be able to formulate a strategy whose minimum objective it to keep the problem from getting worse, with a primary focus on two future dangers.

Two Future Dangers

The first danger is that North Korea will sell some of their bombs or plutonium to a third party. The administration established some years ago an international initiative

(Proliferation Security Initiative) designed to prevent the illegal transfer of nuclear material. This is a good program, but we should never believe that it has a high probability of preventing an experienced smuggler like North Korea from transferring enough plutonium to make a bomb, which is about the size of a grapefruit. To deal with the danger of selling nuclear material, the United States should issue a statement warning North Korea of the grave consequences to North Korea if a North Korean bomb is detonated in the United States, Japan, or South Korea, whether the bomb is delivered by North Korea or a third party. The statement should be as unambiguous as the one Kennedy made at the time of the Cuban missile crisis.

The second danger is that North Korea will finish work on their large reactor, which would give them the capability of making about 10 nuclear bombs a year. We should be prepared to take coercive actions to keep that from happening. The best venue for coercive diplomacy would be the 6-party talks. But we have spent more than three years in those talks with no results, so the talks are a necessary but not a sufficient condition for success. Indeed, the most recent 6-party talks were held [in December 2006] with no apparent progress.

A Credible Coercive Strategy

The United States should go back to these talks with a viable negotiating strategy, which includes a credible coercive element, and which includes significant buy-in from the other parties. The most feasible form of coercion could come from the Chinese and South Koreans, who could threaten to cut off their supply of grain and fuel oil if North Korea does not stop work on the large reactor. This alternative has always been resisted by China and South Korea. But the danger of the North Korean nuclear program is by now obvious to them and they should now be willing to join the United States in a concerted diplomatic initiative. An additional inducement for China and

South Korea would be the concern that if they did not provide the coercion, the United States might take the only meaningful coercive action available to it—destroying the reactor before it could come on line.

Clearly, this is a dangerous alternative. If China and South Korea do not agree to applying coercion, the United States may be forced to military action which, while it certainly would be successful, could lead to dangerous unintended consequences. But in fact there are no alternatives left that are not dangerous. And allowing North Korea to move ahead with a robust program that is building ten nuclear bombs a year could prove to be even more dangerous than exercising coercive diplomacy. We desperately need to get serious negotiations underway with North Korea. And all of our negotiating experience with North Korea tells us that success depends on the diplomacy being backed with a credible threat of force.

If the United States and the concerned regional powers prove to be willing to cooperate in applying meaningful coercive diplomacy, we still could contain this danger. And if we did, our children and our grandchildren would thank us.

| *"North Korea's nuclear test was driven by the perceived need to reduce the risk of attack by the U.S."*

The United States Provoked the North Korean Nuclear Threat

Gregory Elich

The Bush administration deliberately increased tensions between the United States and North Korea that ultimately provoked North Korea's nuclear test, asserts Gregory Elich in the following viewpoint. Based on unsubstantiated allegations that North Korea was circulating counterfeit currency, he maintains, the United States imposed sanctions on North Korean bank accounts immediately after signing a nuclear disarmament agreement. These allegations, Elich claims, were intended to justify economic warfare with North Korea's regime. North Korea conducted its nuclear test in response to these threats, he argues. Elich is author of Strange Liberators: Militarism, Mayhem, and the Pursuit of Profit.

Gregory Elich, "Why Bush Is Seeking Confrontation with North Korea," *Global Research*, October 29, 2006. Reproduced by permission of the author.

As you read, consider the following questions:

1. In the opinion of German counterfeit expert Klaus Bender, what do the experts say about U.S. allegations against North Korea?
2. In Elich's view, what are the inherent dangers in the United Nations' sanctions against North Korea?
3. In the author's opinion, what is at risk if the United Nations approves the search of North Korean ships in international waters?

North Korea's nuclear test and UN sanctions have brought relations between the U.S. and North Korea to their lowest point since President [George W.] Bush took office. Yet it was only little more than a year ago, that for one brief moment hopes were kindled for a diplomatic settlement of the nuclear dispute. At the six-party talks on September 19, 2005, a statement of principles on nuclear disarmament was signed between the U.S. and the Democratic People's Republic of Korea (DPRK—the formal name for North Korea). The Bush Administration, however, viewed its signature on the agreement as only a tactical delay. During negotiations it had firmly rejected the statement, and was brought around only when the Chinese delegation warned that it would announce that the U.S. was to blame were the six-party talks to collapse.

An Immediate U.S. Violation

The ink was barely dry on the document when the U.S. immediately violated one of its main points. Although the U.S. was required under the agreement to begin normalizing relations with North Korea, on literally the very next day it announced the imposition of sanctions on North Korean accounts held in the Macao-based Banco Delta Asia, allegedly because they were being used to circulate counterfeit currency.

Whether there was any substance to the accusation or not has yet to be shown, but there are at least some grounds for skepticism. German counterfeit expert Klaus Bender believes that since U.S. currency is printed on specially made paper in Massachusetts, using ink based on a secret chemical formula, "It is unimaginable" that anyone other than Americans "could come by these materials." The printing machines that North Korea obtained three decades ago, Bender says, are "outdated and not able to produce the USD supernote, a high tech product." He strongly implied that the CIA could be the source of the counterfeit currency as it "runs a secret printing facility equipped with the sophisticated technology which is required for the production of the notes." That the CIA has the capacity to print money does not prove that it has done so. It would, however, have a motive, and the source has not been traced. Wherever the counterfeit supernotes came from, the Bush Administration was already using the issue as a pretext to take action against North Korea. Despite that, Bender reports, "the opinion of experts" is that the U.S. allegation against North Korea "is not tenable."

Rejecting North Korean Cooperation

Banco Delta Asia was quick to deny the charge, saying that its business relations with North Korea were entirely legitimate and commercial. Over a year later, the U.S. has yet to complete its investigation. As long as the investigation remains unresolved, the U.S. can continue to freeze the DPRK's funds. Russian Ambassador to South Korea Gleb Ivashentsov called for the U.S. to present evidence to back its accusation. Yet all the Russians received was "rumor-level talk." U.S. Treasury officials met with a North Korean delegation in New York in March 2006, but provided nothing to back the charge. DPRK delegation head Ri Gun remarked afterwards, "There were neither comments nor discussion" about evidence. At that meeting, he proposed creating a joint U.S.-DPRK consultative body to "exchange information on financial crimes and prepare countermeasures." The North Koreans said they would respond to evidence of counterfeiting by arresting those who were involved and seizing their equipment. "Both sides can have a dialogue at the consultative body through which they can build trust. It would have a very positive impact on addressing the nuclear issue on the Korean peninsula," Ri said. The delegation also suggested that a North Korean settlement account be opened at a U.S. financial institution and placed under U.S. supervision, so as to allay suspicions.

Not surprisingly, the North Korean offers were rejected. By raising the issue of alleged counterfeiting, the Bush Administration sought to use this as a means to justify economic warfare against the DPRK. It was not an agreement with North Korea that the Bush Administration wanted, but regime change, and further action was soon to come. The U.S. went on to impose sanctions on several North Korean import-export firms, on the unsubstantiated charge that they were involved in the arms trade. Then more sanctions were announced, this time against several Indian and Russian firms doing business with the DPRK, along with yet more North Korean companies. . . .

The Ultimate Goal—Regime Change

Any hope for a resumption of the six-party talks had vanished. The Bush Administration wanted regime change in North Korea and could be expected to increase tensions. The North Koreans had earned a reputation for their proclivity for responding in kind: by negotiating when approached diplomatically, and with toughness when threatened. North Korea decided to proceed with a nuclear test so as to discourage any thoughts in Washington of military action. A statement was issued by the DPRK Foreign Ministry, in which it was said that the U.S. was trying to "internationalize the sanctions and blockade against the DPRK." A nuclear test would be a countermeasure "to defend the sovereignty of the country" against the Bush Administration's "hostile actions."

A Conversation with North Korean Leaders

I found on a recent trip to Pyongyang that North Korea leaders view the financial sanctions as the cutting edge of a calculated effort by dominant elements in the [Bush] administration to undercut the Sept. 19 [2005] accord, squeeze the Kim Jong Il regime and eventually force its collapse. My conversations made clear that North Korea's missile tests in July [2006] and its threat . . . to conduct a nuclear test explosion at an unspecified date in the future were directly provoked by the U.S. sanctions. In North Korean eyes, pressure must be met with pressure to maintain national honor and, hopefully, to jump-start new bilateral negotiations with Washington that could ease the financial squeeze. When I warned against a nuclear test, saying that it would only strengthen opponents of negotiations in Washington, several top officials replied that "soft" tactics had not worked and they had nothing to lose.

Selig S. Harrison, Newsweek, *October 16, 2006.*

The nuclear test took place on October 9. There is still some mystery about the nature of the test. The yield was surprisingly small, estimated to be in the half kiloton to 0.9-kiloton range. The North Koreans had notified Chinese officials beforehand of an impending 4-kiloton test, far below the yields of other nations when they conducted their first tests. It could be that the DPRK was trying to conserve its limited supply of plutonium and to reduce the extent of radioactive emissions. The test is widely thought to have been a partial failure, due to an incomplete detonation of the nuclear charge. U.S. intelligence officials and weapons analysts believe that either a nuclear device (not a bomb) was tested and malfunctioned, or that a test was done only on a nuclear component.

The DPRK still has far to go before it is capable of developing a functioning nuclear weapon. If the DPRK wanted to signal the U.S. that it had a nuclear deterrent, then it had accomplished the opposite, with the test revealing that its nuclear program was still in the early stages.

Backing UN Sanctions

It was always the goal of the Bush Administration to win international backing for UN sanctions against North Korea. There were those in the Bush Administration who admitted that they were hoping that the North Koreans would conduct a nuclear test. Having maneuvered the DPRK into carrying out the only option it had, the U.S. swiftly seized its opportunity.

The U.S. won approval in the UN Security Council for international sanctions against the DPRK. China and Russia did succeed in eliminating any phraseology that could lead to military action, but there are still inherent dangers in the UN resolution. For example, UN member states are called upon to take "cooperative action including through inspections of cargo to and from the DPRK." Both the Security Council and the sanctions committee were given the right to expand the list of goods and technology that can be blocked, and the committee is to meet every 90 days to recommend "ways to strengthen the effectiveness of the measures." It can be expected that the U.S. will press for more draconian measures. U.S. officials were quick to point out that UN sanctions allowed the inspection of North Korean ships, and gave the go-ahead for a more aggressive campaign to force financial institutions to cut ties with the DPRK. The Bush Administration regards the Proliferation Security Initiative (PSI), a program said to be aimed at limiting the flow of nuclear, biological and chemical weapons, as the centerpiece of enforcement.

The International Response

Soon after the passage of the UN resolution, U.S. Ambassador Alexander Vershbow and Assistant Secretary of State Christopher Hill asked South Korea to review its economic relations with the North, with an eye to limiting contact. This was followed by a visit from Secretary of State Condoleezza Rice, who was there to reinforce the message. In particular, the U.S. wanted South Korea to halt cooperative projects in the North at the Koesong industrial park and the Mount Kumgang tourist resort. To its credit, South Korea refused to abandon the projects, as both are essential to long-range plans for the reunification of the Korean peninsula. "The decision is South Korea's to make," stressed South Korean security aide Song Min-soon.

Condoleezza Rice's trip also took her to Tokyo, Beijing and Moscow, where she urged officials to implement measures that would sharpen the effect of sanctions. Russian Foreign Minister Sergei Lavrov felt that Rice went too far in her demands, and afterwards commented, "Everyone should demonstrate realism and avoid extreme, uncompromising positions." Predictably, U.S. officials met with more success in Japan, which had recently imposed a total ban on trade with the DPRK. Japanese officials talked of submitting a new resolution to the UN if North Korea were to conduct a second test. The new resolution as envisaged by Japan would require UN member nations to block nearly all trade with the DPRK. More alarmingly, Article 42[1] would be invoked so as to permit military action.

Punishing North Korea

The furor over the partial failure of North Korea's single, rather puny nuclear test made for an interesting contrast with the indifference that has greeted other nations' nuclear arse-

1. Article 42 of the United Nations Charter provides that it may use armed force if efforts to maintain international peace are not resolved by efforts that avoid armed force.

nals. The U.S., of course, has a massive arsenal of nuclear arms at its disposal. There is no suggestion that the established nuclear states should disarm, nor have there been calls for sanctions against the newer nuclear states, India, Pakistan and Israel. The U.S. has even ... signed a nuclear deal with India. In all of these cases, the nuclear programs dwarfed that of North Korea's. Yet only North Korea has been singled out for punishment and outrage. The basis for such a glaringly obvious double standard is that none of the other nuclear powers are potential targets for U.S. military forces. The operative principle is that no nation the U.S. seeks to crush can be allowed the means of thwarting an attack.

North Korea's nuclear test was driven by the perceived need to reduce the risk of attack by the U.S., a real enough consideration given the fate of conventionally armed Iraq, Afghanistan and Yugoslavia. At the same time, the test played into the Bush Administration's hands. The U.S. military is tied up to a large extent in the occupations of Iraq and Afghanistan, but UN sanctions are a cost-effective alternative for bringing ruin to North Korea and its people. How the Bush Administration interprets what the sanctions allow it to do is a question with potentially profound consequences. There have already been indications that the U.S. may go well beyond the letter of the resolution and implement measures that represent a real menace to peace. The UN resolution gives nations the legal backing to stop North Korean ships in foreign ports and waters. But U.S. Ambassador to the UN John Bolton has hinted at the possibility of stopping and searching North Korean ships in international waters, an act lacking in any legal basis. If the U.S. decides to pursue that course of action, it risks inviting a military clash at sea. Japan is considering contributing destroyers and patrol aircraft to the U.S. plan to harass North Korean shipping. This would be seen as an especially provocative act, given the bitter memories associated with the many years Korea spent under harsh Japanese colonial rule.

But then, confrontation is surely what the Bush Administration wants, viewing it as an opportunity for further punishment of the DPRK. Since demolishing the 1994 Agreed Framework, the Bush Administration has gone on to do everything in its power to worsen tensions. "The U.S. never intended to honor the Agreed Framework and did not fully fulfill any of its provisions," points out Alexander Zhebin of Russia's Institute of the Far East. "The U.S. would love to place a bursting boiler at Russia's doorstep. Americans would sit back and watch it explode on TV, and let Russians, Chinese and Koreans sort out the consequences."

> "[North Korea sponsors terrorism] by selling missile technology to the likes of Libya and Syria."

North Korea Sponsors Terrorism

Brendan I. Koerner

The U.S. State Department continues to include North Korea as a state sponsor of terrorism, maintains Brendan I. Koerner in the following viewpoint. One reason North Korea is on the list, Koerner claims, is that North Korea sells missile technology to other states that sponsor terrorism, such as Libya and Syria. Moreover, he argues, North Korea sells weapons to separatist groups and is believed to harbor terrorists who allegedly kidnapped Japanese citizens. Koerner is an editor and columnist for Wired *and the* New York Times.

As you read, consider the following questions:

1. With whom does the Philippine government allege North Korea conducted an arms deal?

2. What are some of the direct terrorist acts that North Korea was behind in the 1980s, according to Koerner?

3. In the author's view, why did terrorists fly a Japan Airlines jet into North Korea?

Once again, the State Department has officially cited North Korea as one of seven "designated state sponsors of terrorism." Yet the Stalinist "Hermit Kingdom" is certainly no breeding ground for the likes of al-Qaida or Hezbollah. How exactly does North Korea sponsor terrorism?

According to the State Department, mainly by selling missile technology to the likes of Libya and Syria, two other members of the ominous list. There is also ample evidence that Kim Jong-il's regime has knowingly sold smaller weapons to separatist groups; . . . the Philippines publicly alleged that North Korea did an arms deal with the Moro Islamic Liberation Front. Such sales are believed to be one of North Korea's few sources of hard currency, along with counterfeiting and other criminal activities.

In terms of direct terrorist action, however, the Democratic People's Republic of Korea [DPRK] (as the nation is formally known) has been relatively quiet since 1987, when it's believed to have orchestrated the bombing of Korean Airlines Flight 858. That attack is thought to have been a tactic to scare tourists away from visiting the 1988 Summer Olympics in Seoul; Kim Jong-il was miffed that his country had not been asked to co-host the games. North Korean operatives were also behind a 1983 attempt on the life of South Korean President Chun Doo Hwan, who was scheduled to visit a memorial in Rangoon, Burma (now Myanmar). A traffic delay may have saved the president's life: The timed bombs went off before his arrival, killing 17 South Korean dignitaries instead.

South Korea also believes that its northern neighbor was behind the 1996 assassination of a South Korean diplomat in Vladivostok, Russia. The killing closely followed a warning from Pyongyang that it would take action if South Korea did not repatriate the bodies of several North Korean spies.

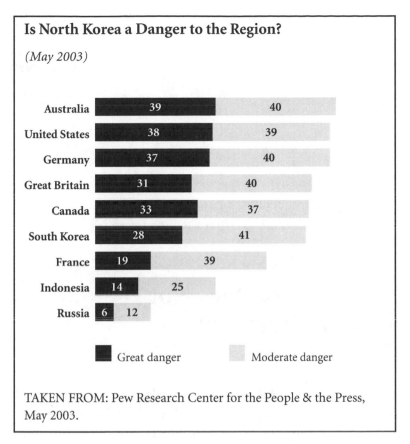

Is North Korea a Danger to the Region?

(May 2003)

Country	Great danger	Moderate danger
Australia	39	40
United States	38	39
Germany	37	40
Great Britain	31	40
Canada	33	37
South Korea	28	41
France	19	39
Indonesia	14	25
Russia	6	12

TAKEN FROM: Pew Research Center for the People & the Press, May 2003.

Every year, the State Department also mentions North Korea's harboring of four members of the Japanese Communist League-Red Army Faction. These terrorists were involved in the 1970 hijacking of a Japan Airlines jet, sometimes referred to as the "Yodogo Incident." They flew the plane to the DPRK, hoping to found an operational base from which they could foment a worldwide proletariat revolution. These Red Army members (originally nine in number) were allegedly later responsible for ordering the kidnappings of several Japanese citizens and spiriting them away to North Korea in the hopes of brainwashing them into becoming Communist loyalists. Japan still demands the extradition of the surviving four hijackers left in the DPRK, but Pyongyang shows no signs of relenting after all these years.

> "Some have raised the specter of North Korea giving or selling nuclear weapons to terrorists. Yet this threat is overblown."

North Korea Does Not Sponsor Terrorism

Ivan Eland

Claims that North Korea will sell nuclear weapons to terrorists are exaggerated, argues Ivan Eland in the following viewpoint. North Korea has not actively supported terrorist for decades, Eland asserts. In fact, he maintains, North Korea knows that the United States would retaliate if terrorists used a North Korean nuclear weapon. Constant threats, accusations, and sanctions against North Korea only increase the likelihood that it will increase its nuclear stockpile, he claims. Eland is director of the Center on Peace & Liberty and author of The Empire Has No Clothes: U.S. Foreign Policy Exposed.

As you read, consider the following questions:

1. According to Eland, why does the Bush administration have no leverage over North Korea?

2. Why does the North Korean regime have legitimate security concerns, in the author's view?

Ivan Eland, "Nuking Our Strategy Toward North Korea," *Chicago Tribune*, February 16, 2005. Reproduced by permission of the author.

3. In the author's opinion, why should the United States be able to deter a North Korean nuclear attack?

North Korea has declared that it has nuclear weapons, a capability that U.S. intelligence agencies had suspected for some time. President Bush is known to have a personal distaste for Kim Jong Il, North Korea's quirky ruler, and his abysmal human rights record. Although regime change in the north is not a publicly stated U.S. goal, the president's ever idealistic approach is to ratchet up the pain in an attempt to squeeze the life out of Kim's tyrannical regime. Although this approach may seem plausible, it's counterproductive.

Because the Bush administration has no leverage over North Korea and no effective military alternatives—North Korean nuclear facilities are hidden and deeply buried, and both Seoul and Japan are vulnerable to North Korean retaliatory strikes in the event of a U.S. attack—it is concentrating on tracking and freezing financial transactions related to North Korea's counterfeiting, drug running and covert weapons sales. Yet such sanctions have rarely been successful, as the ineffective financial war against Al Qaeda should indicate. Governments have never been effective in ending these rampant clandestine activities. In fact, the international economic isolation of North Korea drives its government to turn to such illicit ways of raising revenue.

A Counterintuitive Approach

Because military and economic coercion are not likely to sway this Stalinist holdover, perhaps a fresh counterintuitive approach is needed: empathy. After the neo-conservatives finish screaming about appeasing the human rights monsters in North Korea, a cooler, more rational analysis might discover that a more empathetic U.S. policy would produce better results than threats and coercion.

The North Korean government may be an evil, despotic regime with nuclear weapons, but the United States has faced

Is Terrorism or North Korea the Biggest Threat to the U.S.?		
	Oct. 2006	Jul. 2006
Terrorism	70%	68%
North Korea	14%	16%

TAKEN FROM: Rasmussen Reports, telephone interviews with 1,000 American adults, conducted on Oct. 9 and 10, 2006.

much more formidable foes of this genre: the Soviet Union and radical Maoist China. Furthermore, North Korea is a far-away land that would have no intrinsic gripe with the United States if the U.S. military had not thrown up a containment wall around the peninsular nation. The many U.S. military bases and alliances in East Asia mean that the United States is in North Korea's face, not vice versa. Thus the North Korean regime, despite its deplorable human rights record, does have legitimate security concerns.

Even without such bases and alliances, the United States, with thousands of warheads in the world's most powerful nuclear arsenal, should be able to deter a nuclear attack from the few primitive warheads in North Korea's nuclear stockpile. (Of course, this presumes that North Korea will eventually perfect a missile that could carry a heavy nuclear payload to the continental United States.)

An Overblown Threat

Some have raised the specter of North Korea giving or selling nuclear weapons to terrorists. Yet this threat is overblown. North Korea has not been an active supporter of terrorists for decades, and only politics keep it on the U.S. list of countries sponsoring terrorism. North Korea, desperate for revenue, would not give terrorists the nuclear weapons that cost so much to develop and produce. And although North Korea has sold weapons to other autocratic nations, it would be much riskier to sell a nuclear device to an unpredictable terrorist group, such as Al Qaeda. If a nuclear weapon were used against the United States by terrorists who then melted back into the population, and the sale of the device were traced back to North Korea, enormous pressure would build on the U.S. government to use nuclear weapons against the only party with an identifiable home address.

If the threat of North Korea supplying terrorists with nuclear weapons is exaggerated and small North Korean nuclear strikes against the United States can be deterred by the threat of overwhelming retaliation from the globally dominant U.S. nuclear arsenal, perhaps there is room for negotiation with Kim.

The economic isolation of the north and perpetual U.S. saber rattling make a paranoid North Korean regime even more likely to build up its nuclear stockpile. Instead of economic and military coercion, the United States should take the more positive approach of offering an end to economic sanctions and a non-aggression treaty in exchange for a verifiable elimination—not freeze—of the North Korean nuclear program.

Recently, a similar approach succeeded in dismantling the nuclear program of another "rogue" state. The promise of re-integration into the world economy played a big role in getting Libya to give up its nuclear program.

Even so, because of past U.S. threats, the suspicious Kim might not accept this trade. In that case, the United States may just have to accept that some unfriendly, autocratic minor powers may get nuclear weapons. It won't be the end of the world.

> *"North Korea earns at least $US500 million a year in profits from forging US currency and other criminal activities."*

North Korea's Criminal Activities Pose an International Threat

Michael Richardson

North Korean criminal activity finances the production of its nuclear weapons, claims Michael Richardson in the following viewpoint. North Korea, Richardson maintains, has become enmeshed in illegal activities such as drug trafficking and the distribution of counterfeit U.S. currency with international crime syndicates and terrorist groups. North Korean threats made in direct response to U.S. sanctions against criminal activities is further evidence of North Korea's criminal connections, he claims. Richardson, a former editor with the International Herald Tribune, *is a fellow at the Institute of Southeast Asian Studies.*

As you read, consider the following questions:

1. In Richardson's view, why has the United States refused direct talks with North Korea over financial sanctions?

Michael Richardson, "Of Missiles and Money: The North Korean Quagmire," *Opinion Asia.org*, 2006. Reproduced by permission.

2. How much is North Korea estimated to earn annually from counterfeiting U.S. currency, according to the author?

3. In the author's opinion, what do some speculate is the intent of the U.S. decision to hit North Korea with financial sanctions?

The United States has been applying an unprecedented financial squeeze on North Korea to disrupt what the Bush administration says is an array of illicit manufacturing and trading activity that helps to pay for Pyongyang's [the seat of North Korea's government] weapons of mass destruction [WMD] and the ballistic missiles to carry them.

The success of this crackdown is one of the reasons why North Korea has . . . threatened to launch a long-range missile over Japan into the Pacific Ocean in the direction of the US mainland. Pyongyang is desperate to get the financial sanctions lifted because they have sharply curtailed its ability to do any business, legal or illegal, with the outside world.

It has called for direct talks with the US. Washington has refused, saying any negotiations must involve other concerned countries including China, Japan, Russia and South Korea. Along with the US and North Korea, they are the participants in the six-party talks hosted by Beijing and designed to persuade the North to abandon its nuclear program.

Pyongyang has been saying since January [2006] that it will not return to these talks, which adjourned inconclusively in November [2005], unless the US lifts its financial sanctions. North Korea has denied US charges that it is involved in large-scale counterfeiting and distribution of US currency. Washington maintains that it is enforcing the law and that this issue has nothing to do with the six-party talks. US officials have alleged that North Korea earns at least $US500 million a year in profits from forging US currency and other criminal activities, including trafficking in heroin and other drugs, and manufacturing and distributing fake cigarettes and medicines.

Cracking Down on Counterfeiters

The Bush administration has been ratcheting up the pressure on Pyongyang by cracking down on companies in Asia that it suspects of helping North Korea counterfeit and launder US dollars.

Banco Delta Asia, a bank in the Chinese territory of Macao near Hong Kong, said in February [2006] that it had cut all ties with Pyongyang. It also said that it was putting in place improved procedures to prevent money laundering and would not do any more business with the North.

The moves by Banco Delta Asia are its latest attempt to recover its reputation and revive its business since the US Treasury Department put it on a blacklist [in September 2005] as a prelude to cutting off the bank's access to the US financial system. Other overseas banks in Asia, Europe and elsewhere also closed the accounts of their North Korean customers, after receiving warnings from the US Treasury. These banks feared they would be prevented from doing further business in the US, a key hub for international financial transactions.

A report in March [2006] by the US Congressional Research Service said that North Korea was estimated to earn from $US15 to $US25 million annually from counterfeiting US currency. The Treasury accused Banco Delta Asia of being a front for North Korean criminal activity for over 20 years. The following month, it blacklisted eight state-owned North Korean firms for alleged involvement in spreading WMD and their delivery systems and froze their US assets.

Paralyzing North Korean Trade

Foreign residents in Pyongyang say that Washington's action has virtually paralysed North Korea's ability to trade. Because the North Korean currency is not convertible, companies or individuals in North Korea must pay for imported goods in cash, mainly US dollars.

A History of Criminal Activity

For some 30 years, officials of the Democratic People's Republic of Korea have been apprehended for trafficking in narcotics and other criminal activity, including passing counterfeit U.S. notes. Since 1976, there have been at least 50 arrests/drug seizures involving North Koreans in more than 20 countries around the world. More recently, there have been very clear indications, especially from a series of methamphetamine seizures in Japan, that North Koreans traffic in, and probably manufacture, methamphetamine drugs.

Given the tight controls in place throughout North Korea and the continuing seizures of amphetamines and heroin suspected of originating from North Korea, one wonders how any entity other than the state itself could be responsible for this high-volume drug trafficking. Drug transfers between North Korean vessels at sea also suggest probable state involvement.

William Bach, testimony before the Senate Committee on Governmental Affairs, May 20, 2003.

Nigel Cowie, general manager of Daedong Credit Bank, the only foreign-run bank in North Korea, told a meeting of the European Business Association in Pyongyang . . . [in 2006] that US financial sanctions unfairly hit banks like his that were conducting legitimate business and had strict procedures for detecting fake US currency. He warned that the end result would be that legitimate businesses in North Korea "either give up, or end up appearing suspicious by being forced to use clandestine methods."

The US Treasury said in September [2005] that it was difficult to determine the extent to which Banco Delta Asia was used for legitimate purposes, adding that although the bank was likely to have engaged in some normal activity, this was "significantly outweighed by its use to promote or facilitate money laundering and other financial crimes."

About $US24 million in North Korean assets have been frozen at Banco Delta Asia while investigations into the bank's activities and its accounts by the Monetary Authority of Macau are completed. This suggests that both the Macau administration and the Chinese government are treating the US allegations seriously.

China has not commented publicly on the issue. The US decision to hit North Korea with financial sanctions came at a particularly sensitive time and prompted speculation that some hardliners in the Bush administration want to scuttle the six-party talks and instead try to undermine the North Korean government by imposing a blockade and starving it of funds.

However, Washington has said that it is ready to resume the six-party negotiations at any time, provided there are no preconditions such as lifting financial sanctions. If Pyongyang agrees, it will be a measure of Chinese influence. For the counterfeiting charges brought against North Korea by the US are a frontal assault on Kim Jong-Il's government.

A Vast Criminal Network

US officials have suspected for years that North Korea's political leadership was behind the circulation of phony $US100 bills, known as 'supernotes' because they are sophisticated forgeries. But they say it was only by the autumn of [2005] that they were able to gather sufficient evidence to press charges. In four criminal cases and one civil enforcement action, US federal authorities have made public hundreds of pages of supporting documents. They depict a criminal network involving North Korean officials, Chinese gangsters and other organized crime syndicates, Asian banks, Irish guerillas and an ex-Soviet KGB agent.

In one of the cases, the US Justice Department indicted a leading member of an Irish Republican Army splinter group on charges of conspiring with Pyongyang to put millions of dollars of counterfeit US currency into circulation in Asia and Europe. The arrest of Sean Garland and six alleged accomplices marked the first time the US has formally cited the North Korean government in a US court on counterfeiting charges.

US authorities are concerned that North Korea has become increasingly enmeshed in its illicit operations with international criminal gangs. They say that these alliances for distributing counterfeit US currency as well as drugs and cigarettes are also potential future pipelines for sale to nuclear traffickers or terrorists of material that could be used to make weapons of mass destruction.

| *"The Bush administration has no hard evidence to support its allegations against North Korea."*

Allegations of North Korean Criminal Activities Are Unsubstantiated

Kim Myong Chol

Allegations of North Korean criminal activity are unsubstantiated and encourage North Korea to further develop its nuclear capability, claims Kim Myong Chol in the following viewpoint. Funding its nuclear weapons program through international criminal activity, Kim asserts, goes against the North Korean principle of juche, *which calls for industrial self-reliance. The true U.S. objective of keeping the North Korean threat alive is to justify encircling China with U.S. arms, he reasons. Chol, a Korean resident of Japan, is often described as an unofficial spokesman of Kim Jong-Il and North Korea.*

As you read, consider the following questions:

1. According to Kim, what would peace with North Korea expose?

Kim Myong Chol, "Sanctions on Pyongyang Will Backfire," *Asia Times Online*, February 16, 2006. Reproduced by permission of the author.

2. What has been the net result of the Bush administration's abortive bid to restrict membership in the nuclear club, according to the author?

3. In the author's opinion, how does the Pyongyang administration come across to the Korean people in the face of U.S. criticism?

The unilateral financial sanctions the Bush administration has imposed on North Korea on alleged charges of money-laundering, drug-trafficking and counterfeiting of US dollars are far from a hallmark of the lone superpower's moral integrity and lofty political principles. They are totally arbitrary and poorly advised steps.

Ill-advised as they are, will the financial sanctions produce political fallout? If the hidden real objective of the sanctions is to keep the North Korean threat alive and continue to justify US arms buildup, including missile defense, the answer is a definite yes.

Keeping the North Korean Threat Alive

The financial sanctions serve to infuriate the North Koreans, giving them a pretext to refuse to resume the six-party talks over their nuclear program and prompting them to increase their nuclear arsenal—with the six-party talks in disarray. Second, they serve to allow the US to persist in the policy of hostility toward North Korea and continue to provide *raison d'etre* for an arms buildup, including missile defense. On this basis, the financial sanctions may be called a splendid success.

Successful six-party talks would lead to a peace treaty between North Korea and the US, full diplomatic relations between the two enemies and normalized relations between Pyongyang and Tokyo.

Peace with North Korea will expose China as the true target of US missile defense and the potential threat to US influence. Behind the smokescreen of the North Korean threat the US has strived to beef up its armed forces and encircle China.

The financial sanctions, which will produce the desired results, are fraught with major negative effects.

North Korea is building up its nuclear force at a far higher pace than the Americans expect North Korea will pass the United Kingdom and France by 2007 to emerge as the world's fourth nuclear power after China. The North Koreans will overtake China not later than 2010 to clinch the spot of the world's third nuclear-weapons state just after the US and Russia.

Three factors make North Korea unique. The first is possession of a fleet of intercontinental ballistic missiles (ICBMs) capable of unleashing retaliatory nuclear strikes on the US mainland. Second, the North Koreans still torment the Americans as a result of their victory over them in the Korean War. The North Koreans are still locked in the life-and-death state of war with the United States.

The third is that North Korea is well geared for a nuclear exchange with the US, while the population of the US is anything but prepared for the worst-case scenario of the "day after", despite its status as the world's largest nuclear power. Neither is the Japanese population. Nor is South Korea. North Korea has little to lose in war. However, the US and Japan have too much to lose.

Failing to Prevent Proliferation

Failure to stop North Korea from acquiring nuclear weapons is another reminder that there is no preventing nuclear proliferation. This is signified by an abortive bid of the administration of US President George W Bush to restrict the membership of the elite nuclear club.

A net result is a remarkable decline of US prestige and influence as the sole superpower and world's policeman, becoming just one of the great powers. The US is a far cry from

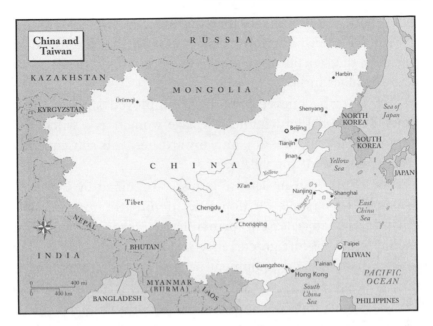

what it was. With all its high-tech weapons, ground superiority and air supremacy, it is being badly mauled in Iraq and Afghanistan.

North Korea and China are both nuclear powers and are in the process of strengthening their alliance, political, diplomatic and military, while promoting economic cooperation. Nuclear-armed and on an equal footing, the Korean-Chinese alliance is applying great pressure on the waning US, hastening its decline.

This represents a total reversal of tide for the Americans whose wishful thinking is to drive a wedge between North Korea and China over the nuclear issue. South Korea is further distancing itself from the US, leaving Japan the sole US ally in Northeast Asia. Japan, however, finds itself split between the two giants.

A Witch Hunt

If the financial sanctions are intended to cut off North Korea's income source to fund the nuclear-weapons development program, it is highly unlikely that the objective will be accomplished. The Bush administration is not all that interested in pursuing the sanctions. Making a scene is simply designed to keep the allies in line.

This is a hackneyed witchhunt employed since ancient times. The feudal lord frames a village woman as a witch, deflecting local criticisms for him toward her, and subsequently keeping control of the village.

The North Korean defense industry is guided by the *juche* principle, which calls for domestic funding, brains and self-reliance in materials. The principle of *juche* conflicts with counterfeiting of foreign currency and drug-trafficking to buy foreign materials and equipment needed for the production of nuclear weapons.

The Bush administration's imposition of a financial crackdown on the Far Eastern country is untenable because it is tantamount to denying that *juche* is the leading idea of the Kim Jong-il government.

North Korea successfully developed a nuclear weapon as far back as the mid-1980s. The end of the decade saw successful development of the ICBM. It is sheer absurdity to call for cutting of funding sources for the North Korean development of nuclear weapons and missiles, 15 years after their successful development.

The Bush administration has no hard evidence to support its allegations against North Korea. This having been said, it is characteristic of the Bush administration to apply financial sanctions on North Korea. Truth is the first casualty in the conduct of US policy.

The Korean Broadcasting Service (KBS) reported that Macau-based Banco Delta Asia handed its documents over to US Treasury Department investigators, telling them they found no proof to back up the US allegations. The South Korean National Intelligence Agency dismissed the US allegations as unfounded.

It is common knowledge that the allegation Iraq possessed weapons of mass destruction, cited by Washington to warrant an armed invasion of the Middle East country, was a deliberate and complete frame-up.

Most US government officials know there is no truth to charges by the Bush administration that Iran is intent on developing nuclear bombs. The Americans told a big lie to its key ally Japan about the US beef issue.

Toppling the North Korean Regime

Suppose one of the key aims of the financial sanctions is to help topple the North Korean government, the answer to whether it will be successful is obvious—no.

The louder the Americans talk about North Korean nuclear weapons and missiles, alleged bad human-rights record, money-laundering, drug-trafficking and counterfeiting, the more dramatically the Pyongyang administration comes across to the North and South Korean people as Korean David, heroically standing up to the arrogant, self-centered American Goliath. It adds to the Korean nationalist credentials of the North's government.

Korean nationalist legitimacy lies in standing up to foreign forces, the Americans and the Japanese among others, and safeguarding the pride, independence, sovereignty and dignity of the Korean people. Pressure from the US is a vital factor that sustains the North's government.

Unlike their Chinese and Japanese counterparts that governed their respective countries, each for up to 270 years, the Korean dynasties ruled the country much longer. Each dynasty lasted nearly 1,000 years, with very few civil wars.

Of all the Korean regimes that have existed in Korea's 5,000-year history, the Kim government is the most stubborn, with the North Korean population closely knit around it.

The North Korean people see a source of boundless pride and glory in holding Kim in high esteem as their national hero and supreme leader. Their dedication is such that they are glad to lay down their lives in defense of his leadership at any time.

The North Korean people find their sacrifices quite satisfying and fulfilling, since the Kim government has built up capability to administer nuclear retaliatory strikes on the US mainland thanks to their sacrifices and has kept the Korean Peninsula from becoming another battleground as a result of its army-first policy and nuclear deterrence.

The Bush administration's talk about North Korean human rights serves only to profit the North Korean regime. Whatever the Americans do only benefits the Kim administration.

Periodical Bibliography

The following articles have been selected to supplement the diverse views presented in this chapter.

Bruce Cummings   "Korea: Forgotten Nuclear Threats," *Le Monde Diplomatique*, December 2004.

Global Agenda   "Fears of Proliferation," October 10, 2006.

Selig S. Harrison   "Did the U.S. Provoke N. Korea?" *Newsweek*, October 16, 2006.

Selig S. Harrison   "The North Korean Conundrum," *Nation*, June 7, 2004.

Paul Kerr   "North Korean Test Provokes Widespread Condemnation," *Arms Control Today*, November 2006.

Donald Kirk   "Decoding North Korea (What a Dictator Wants)," *New Leader*, September/October 2003.

Gary Leupp   "North Korea for Dummies: Basic Facts Good People Should Know," *Counterpunch*, January 5, 2004.

Peter Maass   "The Last Emperor," *New York Times Magazine*, October 19, 2003.

New American   "North Korea Nuke Crisis: Made in the U.S.A.," October 30, 2006.

Ivan Oelrich   "North Korean Threat Exaggerated," *Seattle Post-Intelligencer*, February 14, 2003.

Owen Price   "Forum: North Korean Testing Times," *Washington Times*, October 8, 2006.

David E. Sanger   "Next Question: How to Stop Nuclear Blackmail," *New York Times*, March 9, 2003.

Wall Street Journal   "Kim Jon Il's Bankers," November 24, 2006.

What Policies Toward North Korea Are Best?

Chapter Preface

One of the enduring controversies in the debate over what policies toward North Korea are best is the merit of strategies that isolate North Korea. The crisis in North Korea has been escalating since March 2001, when President George W. Bush rejected his predecessor's policy of engagement. Under the 1994 Agreed Framework signed by then-president Bill Clinton and North Korean leader Kim Jong Il, the North agreed to freeze its nuclear weapons program in exchange for much needed fuel and food. At about the same time as the signing of the agreement, however, U.S. intelligence agencies were receiving evidence that North Korea had developed nuclear weapons in violation of its commitments. While Clinton delayed construction of the promised power plant, he continued efforts at diplomacy. The Bush administration, however, rejected diplomacy, and after the terrorist attacks of September 11, 2001, branded North Korea part of an "axis of evil." The administration considered resuming food and energy assistance as caving in to "nuclear blackmail." If North Korea refuses to dismantle its nuclear program, said Secretary of State Condoleezza Rice, the United States would "further deepen North Korea's isolation."

Some foreign policy analysts agree that a strategy of isolation and containment is best. The United States, they argue, should stand firm against North Korea. "The [Bush] administration has decided that we shouldn't be cowed into submission or forced into dialogue, and that we should actually stand [North Korean leaders] down," asserts Georgetown University professor Victor D. Cha. To engage North Korea, Cha claims, is dangerous "because it means giving the North Koreans things to come back into compliance. And frankly, that is not engagement anymore; that is appeasement." If North Korea fails to come back into compliance with agreements that it signed in 1994, "the only alternative we're left with is really isolation and containment if the North Koreans continue with their bad behavior," Cha maintains.

Critics of this policy such as foreign policy analyst Ian Bremmer argue that "Threatening [Kim Jong Il] with isolation is like threatening a drowning man with a lifeboat." According to Bremmer, Kim depends on isolation to hide the nation's decline from its people. "If [the Korean people] fully understood the harm their government has done them, could see firsthand the living standards enjoyed in South Korea and Japan, and could communicate more freely," Bremmer claims, "the regime might not survive the backlash." Indeed, when cellular relay stations appeared along the North/South Korean border and North Koreans were making calls to people in the South using Chinese-made cell phones, reports say that Kim created a special prosecutor's office to deal with the problem. Critics of isolation assert that the North Korean people themselves are most likely to put an end to the repressive regime. "The most powerful agents for constructive, sustainable change in any society are the people who live within it. Strategies that empower citizens to challenge the authoritarian status quo can create strong momentum for democratic change," Bremmer maintains. "Democracy can come to an authoritarian state only when its people demand it. U.S. policymakers," he reasons, "should find every way possible to feed this demand."

Commentators continue to debate whether isolation or engagement is the best policy toward North Korea. The authors in the following chapter share their views on other policies that they believe will best resolve the crisis in North Korea.

> "The only real solution to North Korea's brinkmanship is to change the regime."

The Regime in North Korea Must Be Changed

James Hackett

Kim Jong-Il's North Korean regime is a threat to international security and must be changed, argues James Hackett in the following viewpoint. Kim's regime not only engages in criminal activity, but also threatens North Korea's neighbors by making unannounced missile launches, he maintains. Moreover, Hackett claims, Kim oppresses and starves his own people. Since financial restrictions, bilateral talks, and aid have failed to stop Kim's saber-rattling, the United States must use more aggressive tactics to change the regime. Hackett writes for the Washington Times.

As you read, consider the following questions:

1. According to Hackett, why did North Korea launch seven ballistic missiles despite worldwide pressure not to?
2. What has been the most direct attack on the United States, in the author's view?

3. In the author's opinion, why has China done little to pressure Pyongyang?

Why did North Korea launch seven ballistic missiles when the whole world urged it not to? The answer is that the Bush administration has been quietly applying pressure [since October 2005] and is getting results. That pressure must be maintained until the regime changes or collapses.

An International Threat

North Korea is a hereditary autocracy kept in power by brute force and a million-man army, which threatens its neighbors, exports missiles, and engages in international criminal activity. Over the years, this has included assassinations in foreign lands, kidnapping Japanese citizens, and smuggling narcotics.

The most direct attack on the U.S. has been the counterfeiting of $100 dollar bills the Treasury Department calls "supernotes," because they are such high quality facsimiles. This state-sponsored counterfeiting has been going on for years, causing two recent changes in U.S. currency. The Banco Delta Asia in Macau, which reportedly has been laundering phony U.S. banknotes from North Korea, agreed [in the fall of 2005] to cooperate with the U.S. Treasury Department by freezing $24 million in North Korean assets and allowing an investigation of North Korea's accounts.

The Treasury warned banks worldwide they should be careful about doing business with North Korea because of its illegal activities. This produced a serious disruption of North Korean financial transactions. . . . North Korean officials have refused to return to the six-party talks until the U.S. lifts its financial restrictions. Pyongyang is hurting, leading the North's erratic ruler, Kim Jong-il, to order the missile launches in a temper tantrum.

The last of the Stalinist regimes, North Korea is one giant gulag, locking its people in, keeping news of the world out,

Jimmy Margulies © 2006 *The Record*, New Jersey

and oppressing its people to the point of starvation. A series of U.S. administrations failed to find a way either to deal with North Korea or cause its collapse. The Clinton administration sent food and fuel that helped sustain the odious regime. The Bush administration goal is to end it.

The rulers in Pyongyang [North Korea's capital] developed missiles and exported them, withdrew from the Nuclear Non-Proliferation Treaty, and [in 2005] said they had produced nuclear weapons. Now they have launched a volley of seven ballistic missiles, including a long-range Taepodong-2 that could reach U.S. territory and which reportedly was heading toward Hawaii before landing prematurely in the Sea of Japan.

The Reaction of North Korea's Allies

Yet, China and Russia oppose North Korea's censure in the United Nations. Post-Soviet Russia sees North Korea as a former Cold War ally and supports it politically, if not economically. China fought a war against the U.S. and United Nations more than 50 years ago to sustain Kim Jong-il's father in power and keep the U.S. away from China's border. Since then, China has been North Korea's lifeline, providing the food, fuel and funds it needs to stay afloat. Less than 500 miles from Beijing, North Korea remains a client state and convenient buffer between communist China and the democracies of South Korea and Japan.

Every government should be concerned about counterfeiting and smuggling, missile launches without warning that endanger fishing boats and airliners, and nuclear weapons in irresponsible hands. But China is not and has done little to pressure Pyongyang. Apparently, it is in Beijing's interest to maintain a buffer state that makes trouble for China's two main competitors, the U.S. and Japan.

A Show of Strength

North Korea wants the U.S. to lift financial restrictions, hold bilateral talks, and provide aid. Many Democrats would do that, endorsing appeasement as the best solution. Democratic Party Chairman Howard Dean says North Korea wants food, fuel and recognition, and we should give it to them. . . .

The North Korean launches show the need for accelerated deployment of U.S. and regional missile defenses. More interceptors and improved radars should be made operational more quickly in Alaska and California. Production of sea-based SM-3 interceptors should be increased, and more Aegis ships equipped with them. PAC-3 interceptors are needed in Japan, and missile defenses should be considered for Hawaii.

The only real solution to North Korea's brinkmanship is to change the regime. That requires continued financial pressure, sanctions to cut off outside aid, leaning hard on China to cooperate, and strengthening missile defenses.

| "Forcing regime change now . . . is very
unlikely to make the United States or
the world any safer."

Regime Change in North Korea Will Not Make the World Safer

Bruce Bennett and Nina Hachigian

Although Kim is indeed a brutal dictator, forcing regime change will not increase international security and could have unintended consequences, claim Bruce Bennett and Nina Hachigian in the following viewpoint. North Korea might take military action to prevent regime change, resulting in substantial causalities and economic damage in South Korea, the authors assert. Regime collapse could also result in civil war, they argue. Indeed, a series of weak, dysfunctional regimes would make negotiation even more difficult, the authors maintain. Bennett is a senior analyst and Hachigian is director of the Center for Asia Pacific Policy at RAND.

As you read, consider the following questions:

1. In the opinion of Bennett and Hachigian, why is North Korea the target of regime-change enthusiasm?

Bruce Bennett and Nina Hachigian, "A Different Axis: Don't Try Regime Change in North Korea," *International Herald Tribune*, January 31, 2004. Copyright © 2004 by The New York Times Company. Reprinted with permission.

2. According to the authors, what have been some of the unintended consequences of regime change in Iraq?

3. In the authors' view, what nations have been reluctant to support a policy of regime change?

I s it time for Operation Korean Freedom? The regime change in Iraq has prompted some to urge regime change in the other two members of the President George W. Bush's "axis of evil," North Korea and Iran.

North Korea is the target of most of the regime-change enthusiasm, because of that nation's behavior: ... admitting and then denying uranium enrichment efforts and nuclear weapon possession, withdrawing from the Nonproliferation Treaty, throwing out International Atomic Energy Agency [IAEA] inspectors and threatening to test a nuclear weapon. These acts have solidified its status in many eyes as an international villain.

Those ready to pursue regime change in North Korea argue that President Kim Jong Il's actions demonstrate the futility of negotiations and the necessity of an international effort to isolate and pressure his regime to hasten its downfall.

The Regimes of Iran and Iraq

In contrast, negotiations seem to be showing promise on the nuclear front with Iran. After talks with the British, German and French foreign ministers, Iran announced Oct. 21 [2003] that it would suspend uranium enrichment and allow full inspections of its nuclear sites, as sought by the IAEA. This and subsequent Iranian agreement to enhanced inspections should reduce calls for regime change by all but Iran's harshest critics.

There is no question that regime change in Iraq removed a brutal dictator from power. But it has also brought unintended consequences. These include terrorist attacks against American troops and their Iraqi allies and an initial bill of $87 billion to the American taxpayer for continuing the occupation and nation-building that is expected to last years.

Seoul Must Survive

What you have in South Korea, then, is one of the greatest examples of human economic engineering in world history. For the country is, notwithstanding its multitude of problems and challenges, a true world jewel. Even in this tough neighborhood of gigantic Russia, even more economically powerful Japan (a traditional, historic enemy) and a rapidly rising China (ultimate intentions unknown), South Korea manages to stand out. . . .

Seoul must survive so as to continue to thrive. That's why precipitous action against the North would be most unwise.

Tom Plate, San Diego Business Journal, February 28, 2005.

The Risks of Regime Change

What unintended consequences might result if the United States now seeks to replace the brutal dictator of North Korea?

Ideally, regime change in North Korea would mean a neat handover of power from Kim Jong Il to cooperative, benign leader that the United States and its allies can work with. Or, it could lead to a quick and peaceful unification with South Korea, as happened in Germany. But realistically, these scenarios are extremely unlikely.

Here are more likely scenarios following an attempt at regime change in North Korea:

- *War.* North Korea takes military action to avert regime collapse or to coerce an end to the international pressure. South Koreans fear this outcome the most, because their country could be ravaged in the process. If North Korea indeed has nuclear weapons, it might use them, perhaps killing millions of people in South Korea. Japan and possibly the United States would also be at risk. While South Korea and the United States would almost certainly win the resulting conflict, victory would require conquest and occupation of North Korea. In the process, South Korea could suffer such horrific casualties and economic damage that it would become incapable of functioning, let alone absorbing the North. The North Korean military, with a guerrilla culture and massive special forces, and a total military many times the size of Iraq's, could well become an insurgent force that would make the Iraqi insurgency look mild.

- *Civil War.* Kim Jong Il's government collapses into factions and civil war breaks out. The loss of central control would leave North Korean weapons of mass destruction in the hands of unscrupulous domestic factions, which could use them in the civil war and try to sell them to third parties. The resulting flows of refugees and the spillover of conflict into China and South Korea could eventually force South Korea, the United States and even China to enter North Korea militarily to restore order.

- *A Worse Regime.* A new regime takes over in North Korea that is weaker than Kim Jong Il's and even more nationalistic, and thus more likely to take a hard line in negotiations to appear in control. North Korean desperation and dysfunctionality would probably increase, and incentives for the proliferation of weapons of mass destruction would be greater. North Korea could experience a series of such governments before probably falling into one of the first two outcomes.

These grim prospects, coupled with the lack of preparation for regime change, explain the reluctance of South Korea, China and Japan to support a policy of toppling Kim Jong Il.

This also explains why the United States has chosen the path of negotiation instead of launching an "Operation Korean Freedom." The likely dangerous consequences of regime change should also affect the willingness of the United States to accept a compromise in talks. Our tough stance may have been a good opening position, but only compromise can put this crisis behind us.

Where Do We Go from Here?

The United States should seriously consider striking a deal in which it joins with China, Japan and South Korea to offer a security guarantee in return for North Korea freezing its weapons program. Washington should also offer subsequent incentives for the North to dismantle the program. North Korea has already offered to freeze its plutonium program. While Pyongyang's [North Korea's seat of government] potential uranium program is a major source of concern, the United States should secure an end to the plutonium project and address uranium later. We can work one problem at a time.

A cessation of North Korean efforts to make nuclear weapons is the most critical short-term issue. However many nuclear weapons North Korea has, the United States will be far worse off if Pyongyang adds the five or six more weapons that it could by completing the work on its 8,000 nuclear fuel rods, plus other weapons that it could derive from uranium enrichment.

The larger North Korea's arsenal, the more empowered it will feel, and the greater the chances that it will be tempted to sell nuclear materials, especially if economically pressured. The United States cannot afford to wait months or years to freeze Pyongyang's nuclear weapons program.

It is certainly true that in the long run, regime change leading to reunification is the only way to halt North Korea's horrible human rights abuses, guarantee stability, and secure the North's weapons of mass destruction. But forcing regime change now, instead of working toward peaceful reunification over the long term, is very unlikely to make the United States or the world any safer.

> *"The U.S. should invest in . . . precision, prompt global strike assets, intelligence and military plans, in order to deny . . . the deterrence value of North Korea's nuclear weapons."*

Aggressive U.S. Policies Will Reduce the North Korean Threat

Owen Price

All efforts to contain North Korea have failed, maintains Owen Price in the following viewpoint. Living with a nuclear North Korea, he claims, will require aggressive policies to protect international security. The international community must prevent the transfer of nuclear materials, impose sanctions, and prosecute North Korean criminal activities, Price asserts. In addition, he argues, the United States must invest in precision global-strike weapons and military plans to deter North Korea from using its weapons. Price is a fellow with the International Security Program at the Center for Strategic and International Studies in Washington, D.C.

Owen Price, "Kim Jong Il: Three Strikes," *CSIS Commentary*, October 11, 2006. Reproduced by permission.

As you read, consider the following questions:

1. According to Price, what strategies are Japan and South Korea pursuing in response to a nuclear North Korea?

2. Why will China be wary of sanctions, in the author's view?

3. In the author's opinion, how should the United States urge restraint among nations who have not developed nuclear weapons?

He tested his missiles on the 4th of July [in 2006] and the UN Security Council voted as one for a resolution against him; he threatened a nuclear test and the world condemned him; and now he claims to have conducted an underground nuclear test. Three strikes—he appears to be down—but will he be called out? How can the international community respond and what can the United States do in the mean time?

The International Response

Since July, we have seen consensus among the permanent members of the UN Security Council when it has mattered, and both Japan and South Korea have reacted firmly, but in a measured way. The immediate rhetoric of condemnation of this apparent atomic test is in similar accord, but the immediate way ahead is fraught with danger.

The United States has repeatedly said that it won't tolerate a nuclear North Korea. Can it allow Mr Kim to call its bluff and then take no action yet again? And if not, what are the options? Japan is already re-examining its constitution to determine if it can take pre-emptive action in self-defense and has heard calls from a former Prime Minister for the acquisition [of] its own nuclear weapons. And South Korea may be tempted to reverse its "sunshine" policy of engagement and pursue a similar course of action. China's reaction will be key and it continues to oppose any hint of military action. These nations have for a number of years been refining a balancing

Enforcing International Law

We need to declare the six-party [China, Japan, North Korea, Russia, South Korea and the United States] talks over, announce that we will retaliate should the DPRK [Democratic People's Republic of Korea] use or help others use nuclear weapons, redouble our missile defense efforts in conjunction with Japan and South Korea, and continue deploying more bomber capability in the Pacific. We also need a more robust program of inspecting North Korean vessels for both WMD [Weapons of Mass Destruction] and illicit materials. And we need a worldwide effort to stop North Korea from using its diplomatic facilities and assets for criminal purposes. Starving the DPRK of its export of counterfeit money and cigarettes, as well as narcotics and weaponry, will hurt the regime badly. The nations of the world simply have to enforce their own, and international, law.

Dan Blumenthal, Weekly Standard,
July 17, 2006.

act. They have provided aid on both humanitarian grounds and to avoid the total collapse of the DPRK [Democratic People's Republic of Korea] economy, on the one hand; and have offered further incentives and disincentives in an attempt to dissuade the regime from acquiring the bomb, on the other. Although there is likely much work for Pyongyang [North Korea's capital] to complete before it has a nuclear weapon that it can deploy on ballistic missiles, it seems clear that the containment strategy has failed.

Living with a Nuclear North Korea

Given the assumption that Mr Kim will not give up nuclear weapons, the following should be elements of the U.S. strategy, while learning to live with a nuclear North Korea:

First, while not abandoning the aim of nuclear rollback, the prime national security emphasis must be on ensuring that North Korea does not transfer nuclear materials or technologies to others—especially terrorists—and to avoid nuclear blackmail. The Kim regime has already sold ballistic missile technology and the U.S. must work with the international community to thwart any future sales of these technologies of mass destruction. Worryingly in the few weeks leading up to the nuclear test, Pyongyang was reported to have strongly hinted at threats to transfer nuclear materials to third parties. In addition to intelligence collection and sharing, the United States will continue to work with international partners on programs such as the Proliferation Security Initiative (PSI) to interdict illegal shipments. Again China will be a key partner in such endeavors as it has an 880 mile border with the DPRK.

Second, the diplomatic pressure for Pyongyang to return to the negotiating table—the Six Party Talks—can be underlined with targeted sanctions and rigorous pursuit of North Korea's various illegal revenue generation schemes. China will be wary of sanctions that could lead to military action and will attempt to strike a balance between demonstrating its own displeasure at Kim's behaviour and avoiding total economic collapse for fear of the potential flood of refugees across its border. It is not clear if regime collapse and economic collapse could be separated.

Third, the U.S. should invest in small numbers of precision, prompt global strike assets, intelligence and military plans, in order to deny much of the deterrence value of North Korea's nuclear weapons and to reassure allies in the region. Congress is nervous about the deployment of such weapons. It fears they would increase the likelihood of pre-emptive U.S. strikes and increase the risk of accidental nuclear war. There is theoretical chance that Russia could mistake the use of such weapons for a nuclear attack. However, there are numerous safeguards—both procedural and technical—that can be put in place to ensure that the increased deterrence value of such weapons far outweighs any risks.

Last, the U.S. should urge restraint of nations that might consider developing their own nuclear weapons in response to a test. Such rhetoric and security assurances would best be bolstered by accelerating U.S. investment in missile defence coverage of its allies in the region.

A Tricky Balance

The nuances of these will be colored by the reaction of China, Japan, South Korea and Russia. Other courses of action, such as direct talks would be seen as capitulating to nuclear blackmail and are out of the question for the United States.

The North Korean test has been characterized as defiant and desperate. Insufficient is known about the reclusive Kim regime to assess the truth, but it would seem that there are few immediate threats left to it short of military action or the sponsorship of terrorism to help it retain international attention and prop up the regime. Either would likely result in a devastating U.S. response. But the likely costs of such a response to the United States, its allies in the region and the people of Korea, North and South, demand careful consideration. Brinkmanship with a madman is a tricky business.

So, perhaps the call should be "two strikes" when Kim has two outs and at the bottom of the ninth. But if the U.S. does make that call, it needs a clear plan of action—pre-rehearsed with allies—in anticipation of Mr Kim's third strike, whether he threatens nuclear use, shells Seoul or gives terrorists nuclear material.

| "Instead of cowering before [President] Bush and his Doctrine [of preemptive war], North Korea pressed ahead with its nuclear program."

Aggressive U.S. Policies Will Increase the North Korean Threat

Robert Parry

Aggressive rhetoric toward North Korea has decreased international security, argues Robert Parry in the following viewpoint. North Korea was not intimidated when the George W. Bush administration listed North Korea as a potential target for nuclear weapons, Parry claims. Indeed, North Korea responded by building its own nuclear weapons, he maintains. The U.S. invasion of Iraq, inspired by the Bush Doctrine of preemptive war, further reinforced North Korea's belief that it needed to protect itself by becoming a nuclear power. Parry is author of Secrecy & Privilege: Rise of the Bush Dynasty from Watergate to Iraq.

As you read, consider the following questions:

1. In Parry's view, what did George W. Bush cast aside in his first weeks in office?

2. According to the author, of what did North Korea accuse the Bush administration in March 2002?

3. In the author's opinion, what lesson can be drawn from Bush's cowboy rhetoric?

Months before [the terrorist attacks of September 11, 2001] and the "global war on terror"—and two years before the Iraq War—George W. Bush tested out his tough-talkin' diplomacy on communist North Korea. Bush combined harsh rhetoric and intimidating tactics to demonstrate to Pyongyang [the seat of North Korea's government] that there was a swaggering new sheriff in town.

In his first weeks in office, Bush cast aside the Clinton administration's delicate negotiations that had hemmed in North Korea's nuclear ambitions. The new president then brushed aside worries of [then] Secretary of State Colin Powell and [then] South Korean President Kim Dae Jung about dangerous consequences from a confrontation.

Targeting North Korea

At a March 2001 summit, Bush rejected Kim Dae Jung's détente strategy for dealing with North Korea, a humiliation for both Kim, a Nobel Peace Prize winner, and Powell, who wanted to continue pursuing the negotiation track. Instead, Bush cut off nuclear talks with North Korea and stepped up spending on a "Star Wars" missile shield.

After the Sept. 11, 2001, terror attacks, Bush got tougher still, vowing to "rid the world of evil" and listing North Korea as part of the "axis of evil." More substantively, Bush sent to Congress a "nuclear posture review [NPR]," which laid out future U.S. strategy for deploying nuclear weapons. Leaked in 2002, the so-called NPR put North Korea on a list of potential targets for U.S. nuclear weapons. The Bush administration also discussed lowering the threshold for the use of U.S. nuclear weapons by making low-yield tactical nukes available for some battlefield situations.

By putting North Korea on the nuclear target list, Bush reversed President Clinton's commitment against targeting non-nuclear states with nuclear weapons. Clinton's idea was that a U.S. promise not to nuke non-nuclear states would reduce their incentives for joining the nuclear club. But to Bush and his neoconservative advisers, Clinton's assurance that non-nuclear states wouldn't be nuked was just another example of Clinton's appeasement of U.S. adversaries. By contrast, Bush was determined to bring these "evil" states to their knees.

A Strong Reaction

In March 2002, however, Pyongyang signaled how it would react, warning of "strong countermeasures" against Bush's nuclear policy shifts. North Korea accused the Bush administration of "an inhuman plan to spark a global nuclear arms race" and warned that it would "not remain a passive onlooker" after being put on the Pentagon's list of nuclear targets.

A commentary by the official Korean Central News Agency cited Bush's threat in the context of the U.S. nuclear bomb dropped on Hiroshima, Japan, in 1945. "If the U.S. intends to mount a nuclear attack on any part of the D.P.R.K. (North Korea) just as it did on Hiroshima, it is grossly mistaken," the communiqué read. [On March 14, 2002,] the *New York Times* reported that "North Korea threatened . . . to withdraw from the [1994 nuclear suspension] agreement if the Bush administration persisted with what North Korea called a 'hard-line' policy that differed from the Clinton administration's approach. North Korea also renewed its complaints against delays in construction of two nuclear reactors promised in the 1994 agreement to fulfill its energy needs."

The North Koreans were telegraphing how they would respond to Bush's nuclear saber-rattling. They would create a nuclear threat of their own. But Bush was in no mood to seek accommodation with North Korea. During one lectern-

The Effectiveness of Sanctions	
Sanctions applied by U.S. from 1993–1996	61
Countries sanctioned by U.S. from 1993–1996	35
Success rate of U.S. unilateral sanctions, 1945–1970	69%
Success rate of U.S. unilateral sanctions, 1970–1990	13%
Approximate cost to U.S. economy of sanctions in 1995	$15 million to $19 million
Lost U.S. jobs as a result of sanctions in 1995	250,000
Lost U.S. wages as a result of sanctions in 1995	$1 billion

TAKEN FROM: Issues and Controversies, "Sanctions," October 27, 2000.

pounding tirade before congressional Republicans in May 2002, Bush denounced North Korea's leader Kim Jong Il as a "pygmy" and "a spoiled child at a dinner table," *Newsweek* magazine reported.

Clearly, North Korea was on Bush's menu for "regime change," but it wasn't the first course. The "Bush Doctrine" of preemptive wars was to have its first test in Iraq, where Saddam Hussein, along with his two sons and top associates, would face elimination.

Worrying Signs

By early July 2002, U.S. intelligence agencies had picked up evidence that North Korea had acquired key equipment for enriching uranium. "On Sept. 12, [2002], the same day Mr. Bush addressed the U.N. about the dangers posed by Iraq, the president met quietly in New York with Japanese Prime Minister Junichiro Koizumi to brief him on the U.S. intelligence findings about North Korea," the *Wall Street Journal* reported [on Oct. 18, 2002].

In early October 2002, U.S. diplomats confronted Pyongyang with this evidence and were surprised when North Korean leaders admitted that they were working on building nuclear weapons. Despite North Korea's public warnings seven months earlier, official Washington was stunned. Many analysts puzzled over what might have caused Pyongyang to violate its earlier promises about suspending its nuclear program and then admit to it. Bush formally canceled the 1994 agreement.

For its part, North Korea issued a press release at the United Nations on Oct. 25, 2002, explaining its reasoning. The statement cited both Bush's "axis of evil" rhetoric and the administration's decision to target North Korea for a possible preemptive nuclear strike. "This was a clear declaration of war against the D.P.R.K. as it totally nullified" the 1994 agreement, the North Korean statement read. "Nobody would be so naïve as to think that the D.P.R.K. would sit idle under such a situation. . . . The D.P.R.K., which values sovereignty more than life, was left with no other proper answer to the U.S. behaving so arrogantly and impertinently."

Bush's supporters blamed North Korea's defiance on Clinton, arguing that his 1994 agreement to stop North Korea's nuclear program was too weak. According to aides, Bush said he would never go down the path of compromise that Clinton followed. North Korea "would not be rewarded for bad behavior," Bush aides told reporters [on October 26, 2002]. Amid Bush's stratospheric poll numbers in fall 2002, few Washington voices dared challenge the Bush administration's finger-pointing at Clinton.

The Lesson of Iraq

What then happened in Iraq only reinforced North Korea's thinking. Despite Saddam Hussein's assurances that he had no weapons of mass destruction and his granting permission to U.N. inspectors to search any suspicious site, Bush simply ignored the U.N.'s negative findings and invaded anyway on March 19, 2003.

Within three weeks, U.S. forces routed the overmatched Iraqi army and toppled Hussein's government. Later, Hussein's two sons were hunted down and killed by U.S. troops, and the Iraqi dictator was captured. Humiliating photos of Hussein being examined by doctors and sitting in his underwear were distributed around the world. He was then put on trial in Iraq—rather than before an international tribunal at The Hague—so the proceedings could end with his execution by hanging, an expected outcome that Bush relished. [Hussein was hanged on December 31, 2006.]

The war's consequences for Iraqis over the past three years also have been horrific. Tens of thousands of Iraqis—men, women and children—have died; the once-prosperous country has sunk into chaos and poverty; ethnic cleansing and a bloody civil war have begun. While Bush may have intended the Iraq war to be an object lesson about the futility of defying his will, some American adversaries learned something else—that disarmament and cooperation with the United Nations are for suckers.

After all, Hussein had complied with U.N. demands for eliminating his stockpiles of unconventional weapons and had forsaken active development of nuclear weapons. He even agreed to unfettered U.N. inspections. Hussein's reward was to see his two sons killed, his country ravaged, and the almost certain end of his own life coming as he dangles from the end of a rope, rather than his request that he die before a firing squad.

So, instead of cowering before Bush and his Doctrine, North Korea pressed ahead with its nuclear program, claiming to have detonated a small nuclear device on Oct. 9 [2006].

The U.S. Reaction

Bush responded to the news with more threats and more tough rhetoric, calling the explosion a "provocative act" and "a threat to international peace and security." For their part, Democrats argued that Bush's Iraq war had distracted the United States from addressing the worse threat from North

Korea. "What it tells you is that we started at the wrong end of the 'axis of evil'" said former Democratic Sen. Sam Nunn of Georgia [on October 10, 2006]. "We started with the least dangerous of the countries, Iraq, and we knew it at the time. And now we have to deal with that."

Another lesson that could be drawn from Bush's cowboy rhetoric is that tough-talkin' diplomacy may play well with loudmouth TV pundits, newspaper columnists and radio hosts. But it doesn't necessarily serve America's national security interests very well.

In a Consortiumnews.com story entitled "Deeper Into the Big Muddy," published nearly four years ago on Oct. 27, 2002, I wrote: "As world leaders have known for centuries, belligerent words and bellicose actions can have real consequences. Sometimes, potential enemies take hostile gestures more seriously than they are meant and events spiral out of control. That's what appears to have happened with North Korea's nuclear bomb program. . . . Potential enemies may come to think that the best way to protect their nations against Bush's unilateralist policies and threats of invasions is to quickly add a nuclear bomb or two to the arsenal."

In the past four years, Bush's tough-talkin' diplomacy has led the United States ever deeper—now neck deep—into the "big muddy."

| "To advance U.S. security interests, the United States should agree to bilateral negotiations."

The United States Should Negotiate with North Korea

Selig S. Harrison

In order to roll back North Korea's nuclear weapons program, claims Selig S. Harrison in the following viewpoint, the United States should abandon its aggressive regime-change rhetoric and conduct bilateral negotiations with North Korea. North Korea's nuclear test was not a military challenge, Harrison argues, but an attempt to establish sovereignty and urge the United States to end its economic war against North Korea. The United States should negotiate with North Korea, ease sanctions, and remove North Korea from its list of terrorist states, he maintains. Harrison, a fellow at the Center for International Policy, is author of Korean Endgame.

As you read, consider the following questions:

1. According to Harrison, under what conditions would North Korea be willing to dismantle its nuclear weapons program?

2. What have sanctions given hardliners in Pyongyang, according to the author?

3. In the author's opinion, what evidence is there that the Bush administration is pursuing a policy of regime change in North Korea?

"You have learned to live with other nuclear powers," said Vice Foreign Minister Kim Gye Gwan, North Korea's chief nuclear negotiator, leaning forward over the dinner table in Pyongyang [North Korea's capital]. "So why not us? We really want to coexist with the United States peacefully, but you must learn to coexist with a North Korea that has nuclear weapons."

"That doesn't sound like you are serious when you talk about denuclearization," I replied.

"You misunderstand me," he said. "We are definitely prepared to carry out the Beijing agreement, step by step, but we won't completely and finally dismantle our nuclear weapons program until our relations with the United States are fully normalized. That will take some time, and until we reach the final target, we should find a way to coexist."

A New Reason to Talk

This exchange foreshadowed the North Korean test of a nuclear explosive device that has prompted demands for a naval blockade or military strikes against known North Korean nuclear facilities. But my conversations with six key North Korean leaders on a recent visit indicated that the test opens up new diplomatic opportunities and should not be viewed primarily as a military challenge.

Paradoxical as it may seem, Pyongyang staged the test as a last-ditch effort to jump-start a bilateral dialogue on the normalization of relations that the United States has so far spurned. Over and over, I was told that Pyongyang wants bilateral negotiations to set the stage for implementation of the

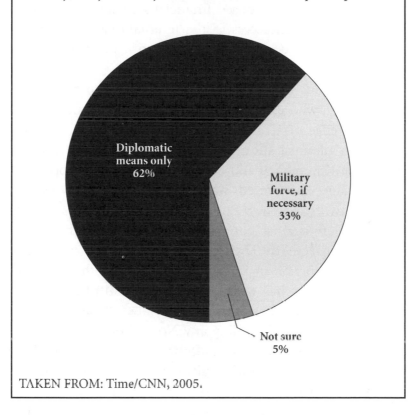

Public Opinion on Dealing with North Korea

Should the U.S. use diplomatic means only to try to persuade North Korea to give up its nuclear weapons or should it use military force, if necessary, to try to destroy North Korea's nuclear weapons capabilities?

Diplomatic means only
62%

Military force, if necessary
33%

Not sure
5%

TAKEN FROM: Time/CNN, 2005.

denuclearization agreement it concluded in Beijing [China] on Sept. 19, 2005, with the United States, China, Russia, Japan and South Korea.

Washington focuses on Article One of the accord, in which North Korea agreed to "abandon all nuclear weapons and existing nuclear programs." But what made the agreement acceptable to Pyongyang was the pledge in Article Two that the United States and North Korea would "respect each other's sovereignty, exist peacefully together and take steps to normalize relations."

A Perceived U.S. Violation

In North Korean eyes, it was a flagrant violation when, four days after the agreement was signed, the United States in effect declared economic war on the Kim Jong Il regime. The Treasury Department imposed financial sanctions designed to cut off North Korean access to the international banking system, branding it a "criminal state" guilty of counterfeiting and money laundering.

The sanctions issue has given the initiative to hard-liners in Pyongyang, who can plausibly argue that the sanctions are the cutting edge of a calculated effort by dominant elements in the Bush administration to undercut the Beijing agreement, squeeze the Kim regime and eventually force its collapse.

To be sure, the United States should take action against any abuse of its currency. But the financial sanctions are not targeted solely against counterfeiting and any other illicit North Korean activity. They go much further by seeking to cut off all North Korean financial intercourse with the world. The United States has warned financial institutions everywhere, Treasury Undersecretary Stuart Levey said Aug. 23, [2006,] "of the risks in holding any North Korean accounts."

Foreign businessmen and diplomats in Pyongyang told me of numerous cases in which legitimate imports of industrial equipment to make consumer goods have been blocked by the banking sanctions. This slows down the efforts of North Korean reformers to open up to the outside world and curtails economic growth. So far, the sanctions do not appear to be undermining the regime, but North Korean leaders can feel the noose tightening.

A Dangerous Game

The Bush administration says that it is not pursuing a policy of "regime change," but the president did tell Bob Woodward that he would like to "topple" Kim Jong Il, according to Woodward's book "Bush at War." . . . When a State Department official told Levey that the sanctions should distinguish between licit and illicit North Korean activity, Levey replied, "You know the president loves this stuff." Robert Joseph, John Bolton's successor as undersecretary of state for arms control, said at a . . . State Department meeting that he hoped the sanctions would "put out all the lights in Pyongyang."

To advance U.S. security interests, the United States should agree to bilateral negotiations. It should press North Korea to suspend further nuclear and missile tests while negotiations on normalization proceed, freeze plutonium production and make a firm, timebound commitment to return to the six-party talks. In return, the administration should negotiate a compromise on the financial sanctions that would reopen North Korean access to the international banking system, offer large-scale energy cooperation and remove North Korea from the State Department's list of terrorist states, thus opening the way for multilateral aid from the World Bank, the International Monetary Fund and the Asian Development Bank, all of which North Korea is actively seeking to join.

Playing games with "regime change" has become much too dangerous and should now give way to a sustained diplomatic effort to roll back North Korea's nuclear weapons program while it is still in its early stages.

> "A continued policy of conference diplo-
> macy and empty threats will give us
> the worst of all worlds: more nuclear
> weapons in North Korea."

The United States Should Not Negotiate with North Korea

Dan Blumenthal

Continued diplomacy will increase, not decrease the North Ko-
rean threat, asserts Dan Blumenthal in the following viewpoint.
The regime has continually broken its commitment to non-
nuclearization, Blumenthal claims, and has received only moder-
ate sanctions and condemnation in response. If the United States
wants to prevent North Korea from adding to its nuclear arse-
nal, he argues, it should not negotiate. Instead, he maintains, the
United States should impose severe sanctions that isolate the na-
tion and should point more of its own nuclear arsenal in North
Korea's direction. Blumenthal is a fellow at the American Enter-
prise Institute, a conservative think tank.

As you read, consider the following questions:

1. In Blumenthal's opinion, what was the international response to Kim Jong Il's missile testing?

2. What are some possible motives for Kim's escalating when he is close to getting what he wants, according to the author?

3. In the author's view, why might China think a nuclear North Korea may not be so bad?

Here we are again. Kim Jong Il is doing what we have come to expect of him: threatening the world and engaging in nuclear brinkmanship. And this time the Dear Leader is declaring his regime's intention to test an actual nuclear weapon.

A Weak Response

[In July 2006] ignoring the warnings of the United States and other members of the six party talks, Kim Jong Il decided to test several short- and long-range missiles. No one besides our closest ally in Asia, Japan, seemed to care much, and the international response was far softer than what Tokyo proposed. Kim was slapped with sanctions prohibiting the sale of nuclear and missile materials. Japan went forward with its own broader unilateral sanctions, and, clearly dissatisfied with the international and American responses, mused aloud about the need for a nuclear-strike capability.

But all Kim Jong Il had to do was wait for the huffing and puffing to peter out. By September [2006], Washington was offering Pyongyang [the seat of North Korea's government] one-on-one talks and "flexibility" on sanctions currently in place to keep North Korea from trafficking in counterfeit money. These sanctions have clearly hurt the cash-strapped regime, which lives off a combination of criminal activity and extorted foreign aid. And yet, Washington's concessions, apparently, were not good enough for the Dear Leader.

Kim has decided to up the ante and threaten to test a nuclear weapon. Another round of threats has ensued. A very provocative act, said Secretary of State Condoleezza Rice. "Bad news," according to the E.U.'s [European Union's] Javier Solana. But why should Kim worry about consequences? U.S. and Japanese efforts to get the United Nations to express disapproval in advance of a test—a simple warning of Chapter 7 actions that could lead to tougher sanctions and the use of force—have already been rebuffed by North Korea's "protectors," as Ambassador John Bolton calls China and Russia.

Looking for Explanations

Reasonable people may ask, Why is Kim escalating when he is so close to getting what he wants? There are plenty of possible motivations. Japanese prime minister Shinzo Abe is set to visit South Korea in October [2006] on a fence-mending trip. A Japanese-South Korean rapprochement would be a major blow to Kim's strategy of weakening America's Asian alliances. Perhaps Kim is peeved that Australia, New Zealand, Canada, and the Philippines joined Japan, South Korea, and the United States (Russia and China sat out) at a . . . meeting in New York on the North Korean nuclear crisis. Maybe the paranoid leader is upset by signs that the U.S.-South Korea relationship may be fixable?

There is also the Iran factor. Kim and Mahmoud Ahmadinejad seem to be studying each other's moves. The Iranian president wants his own six party-like process, which would allow him also to build up his country's nuclear arsenal while extracting all the benefits of diplomacy with the big boys. Just like Kim. And it was soon after Iran was rewarded for its own provocations by an offer of goodies from the E.U. and America that Kim tested his missiles this summer. Perhaps Kim also desires the respect Ahmadinejad has received. The Iranian president got to speak in New York at the United Nations and the citadel of the foreign policy establishment, the Council on Foreign Relations. He was even on the cover of *Time*.

Of course, no one really knows what Kim is after, besides survival, which nuclear weapons will buy him for a while. But he has also learned that brinkmanship and escalation work. Why not continue and see what else he can get, especially from Seoul and Beijing?

The Problem with More Diplomacy

The United States . . . warned privately and publicly that "we are not going to live with a nuclear North Korea." But we have said that before, and we have been living with a nuclear North Korea for quite some time. Besides, what actions will we take to not "live with a nuclear North Korea"?

Proponents of more diplomacy argue that, had the United States pursued a more rigorous diplomacy, we could have convinced China and South Korea, once diplomacy failed, to support a more coercive approach. But Beijing's geopolitical calculation—a nuclear North Korea may not be so bad when compared with the alternative of a unified Korea allied with Washington—precludes getting tough with Kim. And the growing pains of South Korea's immature democracy have complicated Washington's attempts to work with it on the North Korea issue.

Even worse, the "more-diplomacy" argument overlooks the basic truth about our North Korea problem, which is that we *are* willing to live with a nuclear North Korea, because the alternative is a major war. In which case, our policy should be based on the premise that we will be living with a nuclear North Korea until the Kim regime is gone. Such a policy requires first getting ourselves out of the six party talks, so we can focus on defending ourselves and reassuring our nervous allies Japan and South Korea that our nuclear umbrella will protect them.

Deterring the North Korean Regime

We also have other means of deterring the Dear Leader, mitigating his threats, and working toward his eventual demise.

Unrelenting pressure can be put on the trade in illicit goods that keeps Kim's regime alive. We can adopt a more robust nuclear posture in Asia. We can mitigate the artillery threat to Seoul through counter-battery weaponry. We can intensify our Proliferation Security Initiative activities, and place a quarantine and inspection regime on ships moving to and from North Korea. We can also accelerate the deployment of missile defenses to our regional allies. We can launch an international campaign to ameliorate human rights abuses and absorb refugees, and so on.

But a continued policy of conference diplomacy and empty threats will give us the worst of all worlds: more nuclear weapons in North Korea and more alliance problems with South Korea and Japan. The lesson we should be teaching Pyongyang is that breaking your commitment to non-nuclearization leads not to concession after concession, but to isolation, pressure, and the uncomfortable position of having a nuclear arsenal pointed at you.

Periodical Bibliography

The following articles have been selected to supplement the diverse views presented in this chapter.

Dan Blumenthal — "Kim Jon Il, Rocket Man; Time to Defuse Him," *Weekly Standard*, July 17, 2006.

Ian Bremmer — "Toward a Fresh Foreign Policy," *U.S. News & World Report*, September 25, 2006.

William F. Buckley Jr. — "Diplomacy Hits Kim," *National Review*, November 6, 2006.

Christian Science Monitor — "The Think-Twice Sanctions on North Korea," October 16, 2006.

Joseph Gerson — "Preventing Nuclear War in Korea," *ZNet*, October 15, 2006.

Donald Gregg and Don Oberdorfer — "Wrong Path on North Korea," *Washington Post*, September 6, 2006.

Martin Hart-Landsberg and John Feffer — "Sanctions and War on the Korean Peninsula," *Foreign Policy in Focus*, January 17, 2007.

William F. Jasper — "Bad Dealing with North Korea," *New American*, November 13, 2006.

Paul Kerr — "North Korea: Are the Six-Party Talks Dead?" *Arms Control Today*, September 2006.

Michael A. Levi — "Responding to Pyongyang with an Eye Toward Tehran," *Slate*, October 12, 2006.

Abe Shinzo — "5-Way Solidarity Key to Pressing N. Korea," *Daily Yomiuri*, November 19, 2006.

Arthur Waldron — "A Korean Solution?" *Commentary*, June 2005.

OPPOSING
VIEWPOINTS®
SERIES

CHAPTER 3

What Policies Will Best Serve South Korea?

Chapter Preface

Since its inception, the alliance between the United States and South Korea has faced challenges that inform the debate over what policies will best serve South Korea. The relationship between these two nations, and its challenges, began following World War II, when the United States divided Korea into Soviet and U.S. zones. In September 1945, 25,000 American soldiers relieved southern Koreans from hated occupation by Japan. Nevertheless, many resented the American presence and the U.S.-held belief that the Korean people were not ready for independence. Dissatisfaction with controversial U.S.-sponsored elections and the resulting authoritarian governments led to civil strife. The alliance strengthened, however, when North Korea, supported by Communist forces from the Soviet Union and China, invaded South Korea on June 25, 1950. United Nations and South Korean forces led by U.S. General Douglas MacArthur drove out the invaders, but the war continued for another three years, leaving both Koreas in ruins.

During the early years following the Korean War, South Korea and the United States were united against a common military threat—North Korea. Over time, however, the nature of the alliance began to change. South Korea grew increasingly strong, and the focus of the relationship shifted from military support to economic exchange. By the 1970s, South Korea, a nation once decimated by war, transformed itself into the world's eleventh largest economy. While economic ties between the two nations remain strong, recent events have again put a strain on the alliance.

The terrorist attacks of September 11, 2001, "have touched every facet of American life," Alexander Vershbow, U.S. ambassador to South Korea, asserts. In addition to domestic security, many Americans have shown a renewed interest in international security. "The higher priority attached to combating terrorism and weapons of mass destruction, and to promoting the spread of freedom and democracy as the best antidote to extremist ideologies, can only be understood in the context of September 11," Vershbow claims. Bush administration policies that have taken a harder line against North Korean nuclear ambitions, illicit activities, and human rights violations, reflect this new attitude. Indeed, in his 2002 State of the Union address, President George W. Bush included North Korea, along with Iraq and Iran, in an "axis of evil."

Few South Koreans share these attitudes. "Many Koreans," Vershbow maintains, "no longer see North Korea as an enemy, but as a partner in need of assistance and understanding." South Korea has adopted a policy of engagement with the North. The goal of this "sunshine policy" is to soften North Korean attitudes by encouraging economic assistance and interaction. Another challenge to the alliance is growing public resentment of the U.S. military presence, especially among younger South Koreans. In June 2002, U.S. soldiers driving an armored vehicle struck and killed two teenage girls. The soldiers' acquittal in a U.S. military court flamed resentment. In the protests that followed the acquittal, some demonstrators called for U.S. troop withdrawal.

While challenges remain, some observers believe that greater mutual understanding of the attitudes and goals of both nations will resolve the challenges facing the alliance. "Leaders in our two great countries have a shared responsibility to ensure that Koreans and Americans have a good understanding of each other," Vershbow maintains, so that "we will be able to forge an effective strategy on how to deal not only with the North Korean nuclear issue, but with regional and global challenges as well."

The nature and scope of the U.S.-South Korean alliance remains uncertain. These uncertainties are reflected in the views of the authors in the following chapter.

| "While unification seems like a happy ending where freedom triumphs, a unified Korea could be just the beginning of a new nightmare."

Korean Reunification Will Be Costly for South Korea

Bruce Bennett

Korean unification will be fraught with problems for South Korea, argues Bruce Bennett in the following viewpoint. For example, millions of refugees will flood South Korea, straining its economy, he asserts. The South alone cannot rebuild the North Korean economy, Bennett maintains, and would need billions in aid from the United States and other nations. In addition, he claims, members of North Korea's million-man army will find themselves out of work, and like the soldiers of Saddam Hussein's Iraqi army, may turn to insurgency. Bennett is a policy analyst at RAND, a public policy research organization.

As you read, consider the following questions:

1. According to Bennett, why is North Korea an economic basket case?

2. Why was German unification easier than Korean unification will be, in the author's view?

Bruce Bennett, "N Korea Policy Options," *United Press International*, November 28, 2006. Copyright © 2006 by United Press International. Reproduced by permission.

3. In the author's opinion, how can North Korea's military be put to work?

In Iraq, regime change—even when it involved the fall of a dictator whom President George W. Bush called a member of the "axis of evil"—created many unexpected and costly problems. The same thing could happen if regime change comes to North Korea.

The time to begin preparing for these problems is now.

The Benefits and Risks of Regime Change

No tears would be shed around the world if nuclear-armed axis of evil dictator Kim Jung-Il lost power in North Korea. But those longing to see Kim deposed should remember the old saying: "Be careful what you wish for, it may come true."

The fall of the self-styled "dear leader" of North Korea would have big minuses as well as plusses not just for America but for neighboring China, South Korea, Japan and other nations. Like a collapsing skyscraper, a collapsing North Korean regime could cause a lot of damage to everything around it.

In his confrontation with the United States, United Nations and other countries over his development and testing of nuclear weapons, Kim is well aware of the damage his fall could cause—and the fear this generates. In fact, this fear factor is a source of his strength. When nations worry that a post-Kim North Korea would be even more dangerous than North Korea today, their desire to topple Kim cools considerably.

Discussing the fall of Kim and his Stalinist dictatorship is no academic exercise. North Korea is an economic basket case, mired in poverty and kept going only because of foreign aid— primarily from China and South Korea. The United Nations arms sanctions on the North and economic sanctions by other nations could put enough pressure on North Korea to cause a worsening of conditions for its people beyond the breaking point, leading to a North Korean effort to overthrow Kim in a coup.

Cornered and desperate to stay in power, Kim could use nuclear blackmail to demand billions in aid and massive concessions from other nations to keep him in office. Failing to get that, and knowing he was doomed, it is not inconceivable that Kim could make good on his threat to turn Seoul into a "sea of fire" with a conventional or even nuclear attack as a final act of revenge, killing hundreds of thousands of people or more.

A New Nightmare

Then what happens if Kim finally is ousted?

A successor North Korean regime could come into place, but there is little likelihood such a government would have more favorable policies or even be as stable as the Kim Jong-Il government. Continued instability could lead to a series of North Korean regime collapses and revolving door government. With a small nuclear arsenal and a huge army at their disposal, each of these governments would pose a threat of war to its neighbors.

If a successor North Korean regime fails to restore order and prevent economic collapse in the communist nation, North Korea could follow the path of East Germany and unify with its capitalist, prosperous sister state—in this case, South Korea. But while unification seems like a happy ending where freedom triumphs, a unified Korea could be just the beginning of a new nightmare.

Millions of refugees would almost certainly flee the poverty and misery of what had been North Korea for the prosperous South and for China. South Korean experience with North Korean refugees suggests that these indoctrinated refugees would not be easily absorbed into the South Korean economy.

The North Korean Army with about 1 million active-duty troops is roughly three times the size of the Iraqi Army under

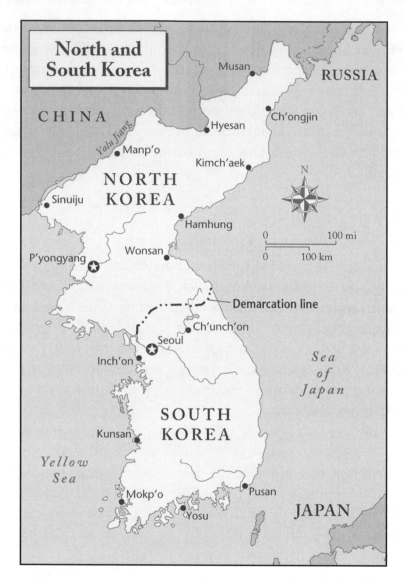

North and
South Korea

CHINA

RUSSIA

Musan

Hyesan

Ch'ongjin

Yalu Jiang

Manp'o

Kimch'aek

NORTH
KOREA

Sinuiju

Hamhung

P'yongyang

Wonsan

N

0   100 mi
0   100 km

Demarcation line

Ch'unch'on

Inch'on

Seoul

*Sea
of
Japan*

SOUTH
KOREA

Kunsan

*Yellow
Sea*

Mokp'o

Pusan

Yosu

JAPAN

Saddam Hussein. A unified Korea would not need such a large
armed force on top of the existing 550,000-person South Korean Army.

But if the North Korean Army were reduced in size or
even disbanded, a large number of trained fighters would suddenly find themselves out of work and desperate to make a
living at a time of economic turmoil with few available jobs.

Following in the footsteps of the unemployed soldiers of the disbanded army of Saddam Hussein, many former North Korean soldiers would turn to insurgency and could go on fighting for years, seeking to strike out against the capitalist South Koreans who had taken control of their country. Proliferation of weapons of mass destruction might be one of the insurgents' few options to obtain income.

The Unification of East and West Germany

There have been many efforts to compare a North Korean collapse and absorption by South Korea to the unification of East and West Germany in 1990. Unification is reported to have cost Germans about $1 trillion, and the former East Germany is still behind western standards.

Yet as bad as conditions were in East Germany, conditions in North Korea are far worse. Some economists have estimated the cost of Korean unification would be several trillion dollars—an amount that South Korea could not afford alone. Huge amounts of aid from the United States and other nations would be needed to rebuild the North Korean economy.

German unification was also easier than Korean unification would be for other reasons. There was far more contact and much more open communication across the inter-German border before German unification. East Germans were not starving in the manner of the North Koreans. And no other country intervened in German unification the way that China may feel compelled to intervene in North Korea because of refugees, nuclear weapons and other factors.

A Plan of Action

The world may not have much time before a North Korean regime collapse could occur. America should begin talks with China, South Korea, Japan and Russia on what happens after Kim slips into history so that the nations can work in partnership and coordination to deal with the chaos of a North Korean collapse.

These five nations need to develop ways to put the North Korean military to work after unification. For example, they could set aside funds to hire the former soldiers to fix North Korea's crumbling infrastructure, much as workers in the Civilian Conservation Corps operated in the United States during the Great Depression. They could create incentives for their own domestic industries to open new factories and other facilities in what is now North Korea to create jobs and spur economic development. And the five nations could prepare initiatives to increase their imports from Korea after unification.

U.S. financial commitments would clarify America's willingness to help bear the burden of Korean reunification and reconstruction. In addition, the United States needs to make longer-term commitments to not move its military forces to areas in a unified Korea where China would find them threatening.

Because China, South Korea and Japan are particularly concerned about their own security, the United States should offer to provide security assistance to deny the effectiveness of attacks from a desperate North Korean regime. Such assistance could involve offering to deploy U.S. Patriot missile units in Seoul, Beijing and perhaps other cities to provide protection against North Korean nuclear attacks with ballistic missiles.

On the civilian side, America should position food and perhaps transportation means in South Korea and China that could help prepare the two nations for the humanitarian disaster and huge number of refugees that could accompany North Korean regime failure.

The challenge America and the world face today in deciding how to deal with North Korea is to choose between bad alternatives and worse ones. In making decisions, it's important for leaders to see the world as it is rather than as they would like it to be. If the problems in post-Saddam Hussein Iraq have taught us anything, it is to expect the unexpected and be prepared.

| "There are several reasons to believe that reunification would not be as difficult for the South as is often assumed."

Fears About the Costs of Korean Reunification Are Exaggerated

Philip Bowring

Claims that Korean unification will be difficult for the South are overstated, asserts Philip Bowring in the following viewpoint. Minor improvements such as the availability of food, fuel, and power will keep a flood of Northerners from migrating South, he maintains. Small improvements in light industry and agriculture will also quickly improve life in the North, claims Bowring. Moreover, he argues, fears of regional rivalries are exaggerated, as ethnic unity is strong. Indeed, Bowring reasons, the North creates more economic opportunities than threats for the South. Bowring is a political commentator for newspapers such as the International Herald Tribune.

As you read, consider the following questions:

1. In Bowring's opinion, what is the received wisdom about Korean reunification?

2. What is the usual example given for what would likely happen during reunification, according to the author?

3. In the author's opinion, what has China shown about fast-growing states?

Looking across the Yalu River from shiny new Chinese buildings [in Dandong, China,] at the secret, dour world of poverty and oppression on the other side in North Korea, I am reminded of what it was like to look across the Shenzhen River from open, prosperous Hong Kong to Maoist China 30 years ago.

So with the latest small step forward in the six-party [China, Japan, North Korea, Russia, South Korea, and the United States] Korean talks, it is worth speculating on whether and how Sinuiju, on the North Korean side of the river, may be transformed over the next two decades in the same way as Shenzhen, now a city of four million people, of high-rise buildings and vast shopping malls.

This is not to suggest any rapid progress in negotiations that at best are one inch forward, three-quarters back. But the talks, combined with Pyongyang's [North Korea's seat of government] slightly more pragmatic economic policies and the shift in South Korean sentiment toward the North from fear to pity for their blood brethren, make this the best time since Mikhail Gorbachev visited Seoul [the capital of South Korea] in 1990 to think beyond nukes and food aid to the possibility of dramatic change and, perhaps, peaceful reunification.

The received wisdom in the outside world, and among many South Koreans, is that reunification would impose impossible demands on the South, with millions flooding southward to enjoy a standard of living inconceivable in the North. It would require Seoul to pump untold billions to bring the North up toward equality of income and lifestyle, in the process causing sharp cuts in income levels or employment in the South.

Public Support for Unification

The Korea Institute for National Unification recently conducted a public opinion poll of 1,000 South Koreans and 300 leaders from political, media and civil organizations. It found that 84 percent of the public and 96 percent of opinion leaders believed that unification was an urgent task; 85 percent of the general public and 95 percent of opinion leaders approved of North-South economic cooperation.

Christine Ahn, International Herald Tribune,
February 9, 2006.

Germany is the usual example given for what would be likely to happen. Its economy is still suffering from the manner of its reunification, with the one-for-one currency exchange and the expectation of income equality of East and West. In Korea, the population ratio (2 to 1) and income ratios (20 to 1) are vastly greater.

A Reason for Optimism

But maybe Shenzhen is a more appropriate comparison for Korea than Germany. It shows how quickly investment and trade can combine with a large, disciplined work force to achieve a remarkable transformation in a surprisingly short time. There are several reasons to believe that reunification would not be as difficult for the South as is often assumed.

North Korean workers are literate and highly disciplined and would respond instantly to cash motivations. South Korean firms employ huge numbers of Chinese in low-income, labor-intensive garment-, shoe- and toy-making enterprises, particularly in nearby Shandong. It would be relatively easy to kick start the North by transferring many of these industries to Korea.

Even assuming that there were no controls on movement of people after reunification, there are reasons to believe that there would be no flood of millions to the South. Expectations in the North are so low that easily achieved improvements like better food, the availability of fuel and power, and access to such novelties as condoms would keep most Northerners from migrating. Giving them ownership of the property they occupy would also be a major incentive to staying put.

The North has a road and rail infrastructure linking its main cities that is badly decayed but is capable of rapid rehabilitation. Heavy industry may need billions of dollars' worth of new investment, but infrastructure support for light industry could be achieved speedily and at relatively low cost.

Agriculture in the North will always face climatic challenges, but access to fertilizer, fuel and machinery to replace draught animals would bring quick gains.

In the immediate aftermath of reunification, the capacity of the North to absorb investment would anyway be limited, and, say, $30 billion a year—not a huge amount for a South with an almost balanced budget and $200 billion in foreign reserves—would go a very long way.

Looking a decade or so ahead, Korea also needs the North's demographics—a replacement fertility rate that contrasts with the abnormally low rate in the South.

As China shows, fast-growing states can tolerate huge regional income inequalities. And Italy continues to demonstrate, 150 years after its unification, that big income differentials can persist almost indefinitely even in liberal democracies prone to redistributive policies.

Korea has a history of fierce regional rivalries and North/South fissures that predate 1945. But even stronger is the ethnic identity that burns furiously on both sides of the demilitarized zone and that ultimately will make reunification inevitable. It will be driven by a sense of common identity, not by an expectation of income equality.

That is not to suggest that it is imminent, or that there will not be huge social and political problems, given that two generations have grown up under such completely different systems. But by avoiding Germany's mistakes, the North is a business opportunity more than an economic threat for the South. By 2020 Sinuiju may look just like Dandong, or better.

> *"Our troop presence in South Korea no longer deters the North. It deters us."*

The U.S. Military Should Withdraw from South Korea

Daniel Kennelly

A U.S. military presence in South Korea no longer deters the North, claims Daniel Kennelly in the following viewpoint. In fact, he asserts, a U.S. presence prevents the United States from acting, as South Korea will not allow the United States to make any military move against the North. The South is now economically strong, no longer threatened by Russia and China, Kennelly maintains. The United States, he argues, could better limit nuclear proliferation if it withdrew from South Korea. Kennelly is a senior editor of American Enterprise, *a conservative newsmagazine.*

As you read, consider the following questions:

1. According to Kennelly, what does repositioning and trimming our troops in South Korea signal?

2. What are the "sticks" in the U.S. carrots-and-sticks approach to North Korea, in the author's view?

Daniel Kennelly, "Time for an Amicable Divorce with South Korea," *American Enterprise*, July 8, 2005. Copyright 2005 American Enterprise Institute for Public Policy Research. Reproduced with permission of *The American Enterprise*, a national magazine of politics, business, and culture (TAEmag.com).

3. In the author's opinion, how can the United States re-mobilize against North Korea without endangering the South?

[In October 2004] the Pentagon announced plans to withdraw about a third of our troops from South Korea, and reposition the rest far away from the border that divides communist North from democratic South. In the heat of eleventh-hour Presidential politics, John Kerry lambasted George W. Bush for sending a message of weakness to North Korea. In fact, it was exactly the opposite. Repositioning and trimming our troops in South Korea is a signal that we are preparing seriously to deal with the danger posed by North Korean tyrant Kim Jong Il.

Sending a Signal

Though Mr. Kerry misunderstood the signal, both Pyongyang [the capital of North Korea] and Seoul [the capital of South Korea] received it loud and clear. The Korean Central News Agency (the ministry in charge of government doublespeak in Kim Jong Il's regime) released a statement about the American move that, for once, was mostly true:

> The U.S. claims that this action is aimed to fill up a vacuum caused by the cutdown of U.S. troops. But this is, in fact, nothing but a reckless measure for putting into practice its scenario for another war. . . . The massive redeployment of the U.S. troops in and around South Korea is in pursuance of the U.S. war strategy to wage a blitz warfare in Korea through a preemptive attack.

South Korea's reaction to the U.S. announcement was also out of character. The current government in Seoul is the most anti-American in the short history of the Republic of Korea [ROK]. It is a left-wing administration that has fanned public sentiment against U.S. troops. Yet suddenly this government issued statements making it clear it wanted to keep the U.S. garrison in place more than the Americans themselves did.

South Korea's Fears

Was South Korea suffering a spasm of nostalgia for the good old days of the U.S.-ROK alliance? Were they suddenly scared that they would be left defenseless before North Korea's million-man army? In fact, South Korea got the jitters primarily because it feared the move was an indication that the U.S. might confront the North—"forcefully" if necessary—over its nuclear weapons program. Moving U.S. troops away from the DMZ [demilitarized zone] tripwire, and out of the reach of North Korean's artillery and tactical missiles, is a sensible move if hostilities might be on the way.

For the moment, South Korea's pacifists and appeasers needn't worry. Its current status as "host" to our armed forces gives South Korea the diplomatic clout to scuttle any U.S. military moves against the North. But with every U.S. soldier that leaves the peninsula that veto weakens steadily.

In the carrots-and-sticks approach we have taken toward North Korea, the sticks are strategic bombers, such as the ones the Pentagon moved to Guam in the weeks before the Iraq war in spring 2003. (More heavy bombers were sent to Guam than were used in the Iraq war itself.) These bombers could quickly be supplemented by U.S. naval power. Any offensive strike against an out-of-control North Korea would thus originate primarily from the air and sea.

By contrast, our nearly 37,000 soldiers in South Korea—and the alliance that keeps them there—are purely defensive. The U.S. land force is tiny compared to South Korea's 606,000 troops, and tinier still compared to the nearly 1.2 million North Korean soldiers on the other side of the demilitarized zone. Yet the presence of these U.S. Army brigades allows the North to hold us hostage, because the North would likely respond to any U.S. air strikes by firing thousands of missiles at our bases in the South. Simply put, therefore, our troop presence in South Korea no longer deters the North. It deters us.

U.S.-South Korea Relations	
U.S. troops stationed in South Korea	37,000
South Korean troop size	600,000
U.S. troops who died during the Korean War in the 1950s	33,000
U.S. poll respondents who want to reduce the U.S. troops in South Korea	30%
South Korean respondents who want the U.S. to reduce its troops in their country	42%
South Korean respondents with a negative opinion of the U.S.	53%
U.S. respondents who have a mostly favorable opinion of South Korea	45%

TAKEN FROM: Issues and Controversies, *U.S.-South Korea Relations*, January 31, 2003.

Getting the United States out of a Straitjacket

The U.S. is in a straitjacket in Korea. Two straitjackets, actually, one strategic, and the other diplomatic. The strategic straitjacket comes from Washington's difficulty in choosing between two mutually incompatible goals: 1) denuclearization of North Korea, and 2) peace in the Far East. Given its irresponsible leadership, a nuclear North poses grave dangers, risks proliferation to terrorists, and presents a likelihood of long-running threats and instability. Yet there is no way to eliminate North Korea's nuclear program without some risk of war. Both alternatives present terrifying aspects, and the U.S. government is deeply divided over what to do.

For the moment, the choice has been made for us. Our current alliance with South Korea—the diplomatic straitjacket—prevents us from acting. South Korea will never let us use our sticks. And our carrots have proven worthless in modifying the North's behavior. Thus, we are currently stuck with a nuclear-armed North Korea. The Clinton administration tried the carrot approach in 1994 when it negotiated the "Agreed

Framework," a sweetheart deal for the North in which the U.S. promised to deliver hundreds of thousands of tons of fuel oil annually, and to build two 1,000 megawatt light-water nuclear reactors, in exchange for the DPRK [Democratic People's Republic of Korea] freezing its weapons program. In November 2002, we learned that the North had secretly continued work on its nuclear weapons program, so the fuel shipments were halted. The lesson learned from this debacle was that the North Koreans refuse to trade away their nuclear program at any price.

Nor do we have any effective stick with which to modify their behavior. The South Koreans refuse to give their consent to any military move. They fight tooth and nail against even the mildest attempts to confront Kim Jong Il. It is their country that would most reap the whirlwind if hostilities broke out. Unfortunately, that has resulted in a pattern of appeasement, which, over the long run, raises the levels of danger progressively higher.

South Koreans' dependence on the U.S. is a problem for them as well as us. After all, if not for the U.S. troops in South Korea, what reason would the North have to retaliate for a U.S. strike on its weapons program by attacking the South?

A Transformed East Asia

Why, then, do we continue to maintain some 37,000 ground troops in Korea? Bureaucratic inertia at our foreign policy institutions is no doubt one reason. For decades, the alliance was a strong force for stability in East Asia. The security umbrella that America held over South Korea provided a favorable atmosphere for the spread of commerce and democracy throughout the region.

But the transformation of East Asia is now an accomplished fact. It is time to shift priorities to an urgent new goal of keeping mega-weapons from proliferating into irresponsible hands. A realignment of our forces and some imaginative diplomacy can help us regain the military options we need as a fallback to make this happen.

And we can wriggle out of the straitjacket that currently immobilizes us against North Korea without endangering the South. Given the right mixture of military-to-military communication, dispersed bases, and forward-deployed forces in Japan and elsewhere in the region, America could rapidly come to the aid of South Korea in the event of a general war, without keeping our troops stationed in the shadow of North Korean rockets and artillery.

The South Koreans Should Defend Themselves

Besides, the South Koreans are now grown-ups fully capable of taking care of themselves. Immediately after the Korean War, the South was a dirt-poor country facing a northern neighbor that was not only much more powerful militarily, but also richer, thanks to massive subsidies from the Soviet Union.

Today the situation is completely different. The Soviet Union is no longer around to hand out subsidies, and China is increasingly inclined to view the North as a distraction from its economic goals. North Korea is now an economic basket case that can't treat its sick or feed its people. The DPRK military recently had to lower the minimum height of its recruits to 4'10"—one chilling sign of a chronically malnourished population. . . .

South Korea, on the other hand, has grown swiftly by almost every relevant measure over the past half century. Its population is now twice that of the North. Its economy is one of the world's largest, with a gross domestic product 30 times that of the North. It has the industrial, technological, and demographic basis to field a military that would rip North Korea's million-man paper tiger to shreds.

It's time to let the South Koreans defend themselves. Then Americans can get back to the critical task of defending our own country in the ways we judge best.

| *"The United States should retain operational military command of combined forces in [South Korea]."*

The U.S. Military Should Not Abandon Its Command in South Korea

Michael O'Hanlon

The United States must maintain its command of forces in South Korea, argues Michael O'Hanlon in the following viewpoint. North Korea poses a serious threat, he claims, and in the event of war against North Korea, success requires a unified command. The South need not fear a U.S. command, O'Hanlon claims, as major military decisions will be made by U.S. and South Korean political leaders. Moreover, he reasons, a strong U.S./South Korean alliance is the best deterrence against the North Korean threat. O'Hanlon is a fellow at the Brookings Institution, a liberal think tank.

As you read, consider the following questions:

1. In O'Hanlon's opinion, what is the latest manifestation of the strain between the United States and South Korea?

Michael O'Hanlon, "U.S. Should Retain Military Command in S. Korea," *Daily Yomiuri*, September 21, 2006. Reproduced by permission of author.

2. How many combat forces would the United States deploy in the event of Korean war, according to the author?

3. In the author's view, what do South Koreans get out of the alliance with the United States?

At their Sept. 14 [2006] summit in Washington [DC], South Korea President Roh Moo-hyun and U.S. President George W. Bush presented a cordial and positive joint image to the world. Unlike the case with some previous meetings, they avoided open disagreement over key policy issues. Roh even went so far as to suggest that South Korea had been imposing a type of sanctions on North Korea itself, in its decision to delay delivery of certain aid after the July 4 [2006] North Korean missile tests.

A Strained Alliance

All of this is good. It is important that, even in troubled times in the alliance, Seoul and Washington maintain some solidarity in their core positions. They must, for example, signal to the world in general and to North Korea most of all that their alliance is intact, that they would still fight together in the defense of South Korea, that they have every intention of maintaining the alliance, and that they will oppose provocative North Korean behavior. Among allies, it is almost always better that any disagreements occur in private and that they be addressed in a businesslike way.

However, we can be confident that the Roh and Bush administrations still do disagree fundamentally about how to handle North Korea. The basic fact remains that North Korea has probably added half a dozen nuclear weapons to its arsenal in the last three years—during the tenure of the two presidents who just met in Washington—and that South Korea nonetheless wants to engage North Korea quite warmly, while the United States is wedded to a much harder line.

Questioning the Return
of Wartime Command

In that context, no observer will be fooled: The U.S.-South Korea alliance is still undergoing serious strain. In fact it is still in crisis. And the latest manifestation of that is the continued dispute over when to return wartime command of South Korean forces to South Korea, rather than keep South Korean forces under U.S. military command in the event of war. South Korea has suggested that command of its forces revert in 2012; the United States is on record countering with an offer to accelerate the process and complete it in 2009.

At the summit, Bush and Roh agreed that the question of when and how to return wartime control of its own forces to South Korea should be determined in a nonpolitical way. That is true. But unfortunately, that kind of vague statement can be used to justify almost any policy. And so far, there is no indication that the two sides will rethink their previous positions.

As Americans, we must strive to understand where South Koreans are coming from on this matter. Their position on the issue seems reasonable in many ways. South Korea is of course a sovereign country, an established democracy, the world's 11th largest economy. National pride helps explain why it would want a stronger security role.

For many South Koreans, their country should no longer be subservient to the United States in an alliance that is designed for the express purpose of protecting South Korean territory. In addition, South Korea now surely has one of the top 10 militaries in the world. Its annual defense budget of just over $20 billion does not rival Japan's, Britain's, France's, or Germany's, and is well behind those of China and the United States. But it compares favorably with the official military budgets of countries such as Russia, India, and Italy. As we have recently witnessed in Iraq, South Korea is often an important security partner of the United States beyond Northeast Asia.

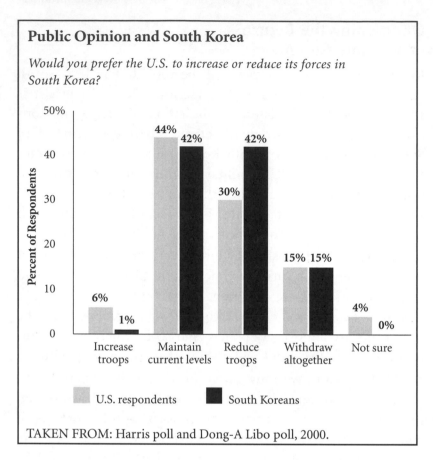

Public Opinion and South Korea

Would you prefer the U.S. to increase or reduce its forces in South Korea?

TAKEN FROM: Harris poll and Dong-A Libo poll, 2000.

The U.S. Contribution

But there is another side to the story, another perspective to consider. The U.S. contribution to South Korea's security remains enormous, and when all is said and done it still is the lead player in the alliance. Moreover, to respect normal principles of military command, it seems logical that someone must be in clear control of combined forces rather than have two separate commands.

In the event of war in Korea, the United States would likely deploy at least one-fourth of its main combat force structure to the theater. Since the total annual cost of U.S. military is now more than S400 billion (not counting expenses in Iraq), this would represent an equivalent value of more than $100 billion in annual expenditure, four to five times the effective contribution of South Korea. South Korea would deploy more personnel overall, but a U.S. contribution of some half million would itself be enormous.

In many ways, South Koreans get more out of this alliance than the United States does. Americans are sacrificing for an alliance that would defend not them, but their South Korean friends in a land thousands of kilometers from the United States. To be sure, the United States would not do this unless it were in our interest. But South Korea has an even more immediate and pressing interest in the goals of the alliance. If South Koreans expect a nod to their pride, Americans expect some measure of gratitude for their longstanding commitment to a distant land.

Whoever commands the alliance, moreover, political leaders will still set the terms of any military operation. The military command system is not a national decision making body on questions of whether to go to war, it is an operational organization designed to execute policy as determined jointly by the South Korean and U.S. presidents and peoples. No U.S. four-star general is going to lead South Korea into a war it does not want.

A Need for Military Efficiency

The decision on changing the command should, in the end, be based on military efficiency. The U.S.-South Korea alliance still focuses on a clear and present North Korean threat. The North Korean military maintains most of its forces within easy firing range of Seoul, [South Korea's capital] has developed nuclear weapons in recent years, and continues to spend about 30 percent of its nation's gross domestic product—by far the highest percentage in the world. War is very unlikely, and would be hugely undesirable—but it is not out of the question. Moreover, the chances for war could increase if North Korea sensed a weakening of the alliance or its military fighting power.

In the tragic event of war, perhaps South Korean and U.S. ground forces could each take separate avenues of attack, avoiding each other and minimizing the danger of a confused command system. However, what would result if one country's forces wanted to move quickly on Pyongyang [North Korea's capital] and the other did not? Who would decide what to do, quickly enough to ensure battlefield coordination and efficiency? Or what would happen if separate U.S. and South Korean armies converged on Pyongyang nearly simultaneously and risked creating a friendly-fire hazard due to their proximity with each other?

Even worse dilemmas could occur with the air campaign. Which military leader would decide how to allocate scarce air assets between strategic targets and tactical targets? Who would ensure control of the airspace so that U.S. and South Korea planes were not mistaking each other for the enemy, or accidentally firing at each other's ground forces? Such problems have occasionally arisen even in the recent international wars in Iraq despite the fact that U.S. commanders had overall control of the operations; they could be much worse if no one were in charge.

For these reasons, this new proposed policy strikes me as a mistake. Dividing commands sharing a common, constrained, small battlespace seems illogical. My own view is that the United States should retain operational military command of combined forces in wartime into the indefinite future, even as Seoul and Washington clarify that the alliance's military commander is subordinate to their combined political control. But if we are going to make the controversial decision to change command arrangements, we should work them out before committing to a new relationship. Otherwise, the United States and South Korea could face not only new dangers on the battlefield, but a weakening in the perceived strength of their alliance to onlookers in Pyongyang and a weakening of our most crucial commodity—strong deterrence against North Korea.

| "The reason there has not been complete chaos in the wake of the nuclear test is because the situation is manageable under the current engagement policy."

South Korea's Policy of Engagement with North Korea Should Continue

Hankyoreh

The survival of the Korean people requires that South Korean engagement with the North continue, argues Hankyoreh, *a progressive South Korean newspaper, in the following viewpoint. In fact,* Hankyoreh *maintains, South Korea's policy of engagement with North Korea has kept the crisis following the North's nuclear test from escalating. Punishing and cutting off the North will not benefit the Korean people,* Hankyoreh *reasons. Engagement, on the other hand, increases cooperation and encourages reform and openness, necessary conditions of a peaceful reunification with the North,* Hankyoreh *asserts.*

As you read, consider the following questions:

1. In the opinion of *Hankyoreh*, why is it dangerous for North Korea and the United States to think that they are the primary players on the nuclear issue?

Hankyoreh, "South Korea Still Has a Leadership Role to Play," October 11, 2006. Reproduced by permission.

2. Why is it rational for the United States to exclude a military response to the North's nuclear test, according to the author?

3. In the author's opinion, why must disciplinary action against North Korea be considered very carefully?

The aftereffects of North Korea's nuclear test [on October 9, 2006]—and how long they last—will be determined by how the North and the countries involved handle the situation from this point on. The worst scenario would be one in which a hard-line response escalates things to the point of catastrophe. That kind of scenario must not be allowed to unfold. Certainly, one can imagine that tensions would be increased right now. But a situation in which the differences between the sides are so great that compromise becomes impossible unless one side gives in completely could easily lead to catastrophe, as well. All the more so with North Korea and the United States, each thinking they are the main players on this issue. Leaving things like that is a choice that must be avoided.

The Most Realistic Choice

The best scenario would be to achieve compromise in a way that turns a bad situation into something good before the crisis further deteriorates. This is also the most realistic choice available. Naturally, there is little room for immediate compromise, since the North's provocative nuclear test has angered concerned countries and because Pyongyang [the seat of North Korea's government] is making wild demands. The North's ambassador to the United Nations said the test "is a response to more than half a century of hostile policy toward [North] Korea by the U.S.", and that instead of announcing "useless resolutions and chairman's statements," the U.N. should instead "be congratulating us." Pyongyang needs to quit with the bravado and look reality straight in the face so as to keep from becoming further isolated.

The U.S. administration is being relatively calm about the announced test. In his statement in response, President George W. Bush condemned the test and called for an immediate response by the U.N. Security Council [UNSC], but at the same time he spoke of the need for a diplomatic solution and for resuming the six-party talks. What that means is that he is excluding a military response and will place greater priority on actions together with the international community instead of having the U.S. act alone. Even given the fact that the U.S. has its hands tied in the Middle East, it is rational on the part of Washington [D.C.] to state clear diplomatic goals instead of suggesting an armed conflict that could be ruinous.

Diplomacy in Stages Toward a Solution

There are an infinite number of suggestions as to what kind of diplomatic solution should be attempted. Shortly after the announced test, the U.S. submitted to the UNSC a draft resolution calling for all of the North's international financial transactions to be halted and to allow for the inspection of any ship entering or leaving North Korean waters suspected of carrying nuclear material or other weapons of mass destruction. The draft invokes Article VII of the U.N. Charter, opening the way for possible military action. This thus may be interpreted as the U.S. calling for a sea blockade. Instead of forcing the North to recognize its mistakes and come to the table, this could make the situation quickly take a turn for the worse and threaten the very possibility for a diplomatic solution. That is why disciplinary action must be considered very carefully, even if such measures are to be included in a UNSC resolution. Low-intensity action acceptable to all nations should be adopted first, and then the U.N. can move to the next stage depending on the North's actions. It would be a solution in stages.

South Korea has to continue [to] play an independent role, one that increases the likelihood of dialogue, while it

continues to work with the international community. Looking back, on not one occasion has the U.S. or North Korea been the first to come to the negotiation table. It was South Korea, through its "profound proposal" [in 2005], that got the six-party talks restarted and brought about the September 19 [2005] Joint Statement in Beijing [China], South Korea should have strengthened its leadership role this past spring [2006], when rumors of a North Korean missile test first began. But the government, not wanting to offend hard-liners in Korea and abroad, lost that opportunity, and so bears some degree of responsibility for the recent nuclear test. It was irresponsible for President Roh to say "Korea's role has shrunk."

Policy of Engagement Must Not Be Abandoned

The accusations about the engagement policy toward Pyongyang miss the mark. The current government's policy of engagement developed out of former president Kim Dae-jung's "Sunshine" policy. Its goal is to build a foundation for peaceful reunification by indirectly encouraging the North to move towards reform and openness by increasing cross-border exchange through reconciliation and cooperative programs. The main opposition Grand National Party's claim that this policy caused the nuclear test can only be because it has misunderstood the policy to be a panacea of some sort, or because the party wants to distort things for its own political advantage. It is precisely due to the engagement policy making progress in areas of economic cooperation and exchange that there have been calls for relations with the North to include political and military contact, as well. The reason there has not been complete chaos in the wake of the nuclear test is because the situation is manageable under the current engagement policy.

Calls for the private-led Gaeseong (Kaesong) Industrial Park and Mt. Geumgang (Kumgang) tourism project to be halted are also being made out of haste. Money paid to North Korean workers at the industrial park amounts to mere billions of won, but the value of the enterprise is far greater when you consider how it contributes to the lessening of tensions and the increase in economic exchange. It is shortsighted to demand the South put an end to the industrial complex in order to make economic sanctions more effective, as that view fails to take into account that the North's military moved north of the complex and would move back down to the demilitarized zone if the operation were to be shut down. Perhaps nothing can be done about the fact that cooperation and nongovernmental exchange are going to be hurt by this nuclear test, but even so, the government needs to be careful about initiating action in response.

There's no way to know exactly what Pyongyang's intentions are, but there is also no reason to cut off North-South relations. The effort to resolve the nuclear issue peacefully and not just punish the North for its test must continue, if only for the sake of guaranteeing the survival of the Korean people. South Korea needs to be changing the direction of how this unfolds little by little, and not just following along.

"The South Koreans, and increasingly their government, are finding it impossible to pretend that sunshine is the best policy."

South Korea's Policy of Engagement with North Korea Is Not Working

Gregory Rodriguez

Engagement with North Korea is not working for the South, asserts Gregory Rodriguez in the following viewpoint. The goal of South Korean engagement and peaceful resolution of the conflict with the North was to demonstrate the South's independence, Rodriguez maintains. However, he claims, the North's blatant brinkmanship has instead proven to be an embarrassment for the South. Continuing engagement without reciprocity has failed to provide the South with any benefits, he argues. Rodriguez is a fellow at the New American Foundation, a centrist think tank.

As you read, consider the following questions:

1. According to Rodriguez, how have South Korean attitudes toward North Korea changed since the Cold War?

2. In the author's view, what has been the result of softening South Korean attitudes toward the North?

3. In the author's opinion, how did North Korea respond to the South's demand that it return to the six-party talks?

While much of the world is fixated on the conflict in the Middle East, there is a whole other drama playing out on the Korean peninsula that is just as crucial to global stability. [The July 2006] U.N. Security Council resolution condemning North Korea's nuclear ambitions has not only ratcheted up tensions in the region, it is forcing South Korea to rethink its "sunshine policy" of peaceful engagement with the North. After eight years of rapprochement with the government of Kim Jong Il, a growing number of South Koreans are wondering whether the North Korean dictator hasn't been abusing their trust.

Understanding South Korean Attitudes

To understand South Koreans' tortured attitudes toward the rogue nation on the northern side of the most heavily armed border on the planet, it helps to watch *Spy Girl*, a silly Romeo-and-Juliet-style 2004 Korean teen movie.

Hyo-jin, a fetching young North Korean spy, is sent across the demilitarized zone to capture a renegade agent who has embezzled money from the North Korean government. But while working undercover at a Burger King, she falls in love with a South Korean boy about to head off to his mandatory military service. Theirs is a love cursed by the harsh realities of geopolitics.

Only a decade earlier, making a spy into a heroine would have been considered tantamount to treason. But since the 1990s, younger generations of South Koreans have developed a more sympathetic—yet still deeply conflicted—view of their national doppelganger.

Products of an economically thriving and democratic nation, these generations resent their nation's military dependence on the United States, and they see the peaceful resolution of conflict with North Korea as an opportunity to assert their independence. Whereas, during the Cold War, South Korean politicians leveraged the North Korean threat to secure largesse from the U.S., today younger, more liberal pols stress their nation's ability to solve the peninsular standoff on its own, through economic and cultural exchange.

Not surprisingly, as attitudes toward North Korea have softened, anti-American sentiment has increased. President Bush's inclusion of North Korea in his 2002 "axis of evil" speech was understood by many as an unwelcome intrusion into South Korea's domestic politics and an attempt to undermine the sunshine policy.

By 2003, half of South Koreans—and 71% of those aged 18 to 29—had an unfavorable view of the U.S. But this growing disdain for their ally is as complicated as their sympathy for their enemy. A 2004 poll found that 89% of South Koreans still trusted that the United States would "contribute military forces to reverse the aggression if North Korea were to attack South Korea."

A Hard Shake

Most of this got a hard shake earlier [in July 2006] when North Korea test-fired at least six missiles into the Sea of Japan. Many saw the act less as a threat than an embarrassment. Instead of fear for their lives, the saber rattling evoked a fear that North Korean bravado reflects badly on them.

"We have an identity as citizens of South Korea," says Kim Tae-hyun, professor of International Relations at Chung-Ang University, "but we also feel part of a broader Korean nation."

Yet Pyongyang's [North Korea's seat of government] recent brinksmanship has also caused a profound shift in public opinion, and one that reflects a less sympathetic, more aggres-

A Strength Has Become a Weakness

What has long been regarded as one of the sunshine policy's key strengths—the separation of economic and humanitarian aid from political progress—has evidently become one of its key weaknesses. Such a separation has meant that North Korea is free to obtain the maximum economic assistance from the South, while under no real obligation to show progress on issues such as divided families. Although South Korea has followed the precepts of "sunshine" to demonstrate Seoul's good will toward Pyongyang, North Korea has consistently and somewhat successfully exploited this element to obtain the maximum in rewards at the lowest perceived risk to its hold on power.

James A. Foley, World Affairs, *Spring 2003.*

sive state of mind. A recent survey revealed that the percentage of South Koreans who believe their country should support the U.S. government's hard line toward North Korea has nearly doubled ... from 20% in 2002 to 37% today. Meanwhile, there are also signs that the public is less willing to send aid to North Korea if the receiving nation doesn't show greater signs of reciprocity.

So far, the center-left government of President Roh Moohyun has been reluctant to toe a harder line. Last week [July 2006], in nearly the same breath as he deplored North Korea's "wrong behavior," Roh warned against overreacting to the North's missile tests.

Still, in the face of growing international impatience with North Korea, the South was obliged to demand that Pyongyang return to the six-party talks on North Korea's nuclear weapons program. When North Korea refused, the South suspended all food aid. . . . The North retaliated by canceling the

6-year-old program that reunites families that have been divided since the political partition of the peninsula in 1948.

Try as they might, the South Koreans, and increasingly their government, are finding it impossible to pretend that sunshine is the best policy. They may desperately want a storybook ending, but it's becoming increasingly clear that their romance with the North is unrequited. And the end of the affair only intensifies their 50-year-long national identity crisis.

Periodical Bibliography

The following articles have been selected to supplement the diverse views presented in this chapter.

Christine Ahn
"Reunification Is on the March," *International Herald Tribune*, February 9, 2006.

B.B. Bell
"The Model for Peace & Democracy in the 21st Century," *Army*, October 2006.

Christian Caryl & B.J. Lee
"Clouds on the Horizon; The 'Sunshine Policy' Is Slowly Driving a Wedge Between the United States and South Korea," *Newsweek*, June 26, 2006.

Chien-peng Chung
"Democratization in South Korea and Inter-Korean Relations," *Pacific Affairs*, spring 2003.

Economist
"Awkward Bedfellows; South Korea and America," September 9, 2006.

Zusha Elinson
"South Korea Coming up Quickly?" *Recorder*, November 13, 2006.

John Feffer and Emily Schwartz Greco
"Slow Motion Reunification," *Boston Globe*, June 10, 2005.

Norman Friedman
"An Independent Role for South Korea?" United States Naval Institute Proceedings, November 2006.

Shin Jae Hoon
"'Protect Regime Now, Feed People Later,'" *Yale Global*, October 10, 2005.

Andrei Lankov
"Why N Korea's Neighbors Soft-Pedal Sanctions," *Asia Times*, November 29, 2006.

Choe Sang-Hun
"Seoul Seeks Wartime Control over Its Army from US," *International Herald Tribune*, August 10, 2006.

Michael S. Serrill
"Seoul Gives the North a Power Boost," *Business Week*, July 25, 2005.

Democracy and Human Rights in North and South Korea

Chapter Preface

While many regimes may threaten human rights, few also represent a threat to global security. The threat to human rights posed by North Korea is consequently complicated by the nation's development of nuclear weapons. Thus, one of the controversies in the debate over the state of human rights in North Korea is how best to address the problem when the nation also poses a nuclear threat. While some analysts argue that regime change is necessary to promote human rights and put an end to North Korea's nuclear threat, others contend that such a policy would further threaten the human rights of the North Korean people.

After the collapse of the Soviet Union, the death of North Korean leader Kim Il Sung, and a devastating North Korean famine, many believed that North Korea would open its economy, improve its human rights record, and abandon its quest to conquer South Korea. However, Kim Jong Il, the son of Kim Il Sung and his successor, realized that such reform would mean the end of his empire. Diplomatic efforts by the administrations of Presidents Bill Clinton and George W. Bush failed to put an end to his repressive regime, and Kim Jong Il has consistently broken his promises to improve human rights or end North Korea's nuclear weapons program.

According to some commentators, replacing the regime of Kim Jong Il would be the best strategy to protect human rights and end the nation's nuclear threat. Foreign policy analyst Nicholas Eberstadt maintains, "American policy should be actively engaged in planning for a successful transition to a post-Kim Jong Il Korea." Efforts to trade aid for human rights reform and nuclear disarmament, these analysts claim, will continue to meet with failure. Author Jasper Becker asserts, "There are those . . . who think that such a deal would be the best way to reduce tensions and to wean Pyongyang [North

Korea's capital] off the habits of a rogue state. But the analysis is flawed." Eberstadt agrees, "We are exceedingly unlikely to talk—or to bribe—the current North Korean government out of its nuclear quest. Talk and bribery have been tried for nearly 15 years—with miserable results."

Others contend that regime change will only exacerbate the human rights problem in North Korea. According to professor Kenneth Liebenthal, "A coup by the military or police in North Korea could topple Mr. Kim only to replace him with another dictator. . . . The human rights situation in the North would not improve and there is no reason to believe that these individuals would prove more sensible than Mr. Kim has been." Opponents of regime change are also anxious that such a result would increase the likelihood of military intervention. Foreign policy analyst John Feffer maintains that like Iraq and Vietnam, "the Bush administration's approach to North Korea[n] human rights may well put the intended beneficiaries at greater risk in order to achieve a larger and putatively nobler cause." Feffer argues, "Inconsistent and hypocritical, the United States has become evangelical in its policy on North Korean human rights. . . . They will flirt with apocalypse to get the rapture of regime change, and North Koreans—who have suffered so much already—will bear the brunt of it."

Not unlike the controversies surrounding democracy and human rights in North and South Korea that the authors in the following chapter explore, the debate over whether regime change will promote North Korean human rights continues.

> *"Public debate may be a positive devel-*
> *opment for the South, but . . . such free-*
> *doms . . . have actually allowed the two*
> *Koreas to draw closer together."*

South Korean Democracy Benefits Both Koreas

Balbina Y. Hwang

While democratization has brought the two Koreas closer to-
gether, asserts Balbina Y. Hwang in the following viewpoint, it
has alienated relations with the United States, which takes a
harder line toward North Korea. The U.S.-inspired freedoms that
encourage public debate over how best to respond to the North
Korean threat also allow for the airing of pro-North Korean
views, Hwang claims. Nevertheless, she asserts, both the United
States and South Korea continue to share common goals. Hwang
is an Asian policy analyst for the Heritage Foundation, a conser-
vative think tank.

As you read, consider the following questions:

1. According to Hwang, why have geopolitical concerns
   always been an integral part of every Korean citizen's
   life?

Balbina Y. Hwang, "Democracy Evolves in South Korea," *Far Eastern Economic Re-view*, July/August 2006. Reprinted with permission of *Far Eastern Economic Review*, conveyed through Copyright Clearance Center, Inc.

2. In the author's opinion, how do Korean and U.S. strategic thinking differ?

3. What evidence does the author provide of the South's dominance over the North?

In the nationwide elections held in south Korea in late May [2006], the main opposition Grand National Party [GNP] achieved an overwhelming victory, signaling a strong public vote of no-confidence for President Roh Moo Hyun and his embattled Uri Party.[1] This election was considered critical to the future of the Roh administration, as not only a public verdict on his embattled domestic policies, but all his controversial foreign-policy stances, including engagement of North Korea, challenge of traditional alliance relations with the United States, and antagonistic stance toward Japan.

Thus, the significance of the election defeat was not lost on the governments in Washington, Tokyo and Pyongyang [the capital of Korea]. All three are experiencing uncertain relations with the Roh administration, so these foreign governments consider the outcome as an important political barometer for the December 2007 presidential elections and the future leadership of South Korea. In addition, the GNP victory is viewed as a blow to Mr. Roh's determination to pursue full engagement of North Korea despite strong U.S. and Japanese skepticism, and could signal the possibility of improved relations with Washington and Tokyo.

The conservative GNP—which holds the majority of seats in the National Assembly—had been waiting for this opportunity to win back the popular mandate. It achieved an overwhelming victory by securing 12 of 16 provincial governor-

1. Roh was elected to a five-year term in February 2003. On March 12, 2004, he was impeached for illegal electioneering, and his own Uri Party soundly defeated the opposition parties (including the Grand National Party) in elections the following month. The impeachment was then overturned in May by the Korean Constitutional Court, which ruled the infraction was too minor to warrant impeachment, and Roh remained in power.

ships and mayoral seats, including the mayorships of Seoul—in many cases by a margin as large as two to one.

But any assumption that the GNP will get a mandate to make significant changes to existing national and foreign policies may be premature. Despite receiving a strong boost from the public, the burden of producing solid policy alternatives to the ruling Uri has actually increased.

Public Dissatisfaction

The Korean public has become increasingly dissatisfied with the Roh government on a diverse range of domestic policies, including questionable social reform measures such as revamping of the education system. Mr. Roh's efforts to overhaul the rigid system ended up producing counter-productive results that has angered parents, pupils and teachers alike.

National economic performance has also suffered during Roh's administration, with real GDP [gross domestic product] growth in 2005 slowing to 4%, down from the 5% recorded in 2004. Middle-class disgruntlement has also grown as a result of Mr. Roh's failure to curb rapidly increasing housing prices despite introduction of antispeculation measures. Overall, public dissatisfaction stems from the fact that Mr. Roh pledged to promote greater equity across Korean society, but his policies seem to have had the opposite effect, increasing the rich-poor divide.

On the foreign-policy front as well, there is widespread discontent with the Roh administration's policies that support reconciliation with North Korea despite lack of reciprocity, insistence on greater equality in relations with the U.S., and stances that have increased friction with Japan. While a substantial portion of the South Korean public prefers engagement over confrontation with North Korea, even the engagers are growing increasingly skeptical of policies that have seemingly produced little tangible results in altering North Korea's hostile attitudes. Similarly, in terms of relations with the U.S.

and Japan, although the majority of South Koreans desire greater independence from these two countries, they are questioning the wisdom of doing so at the cost of damaging critical relationships.

The defeat of Uri is in some ways an opportunity for the party to regroup and regain credibility before the December 2007 presidential race and national elections in April 2008. In the process, however, infighting both within the party and with the opposition is likely to become nastier, which will only serve to further polarize the political process.

And while it may be tempting for Mr. Roh's critics to view these election results as a rejection of the president's leadership, particularly in the foreign-policy arena, in reality there is likely to be little change in Seoul's [South Korea's capital] orientation either toward North Korea or the United States. This is due to the Blue House's [the South Korean presidential residence] increasing isolation from the rest of the administration, as well as Roh's determination to pursue policies even without a clear public mandate. The failure of a previous impeachment effort has essentially given him free rein for the duration of his term. This is also an indication that despite the fact that a vibrant democratic process has taken root in South Korea, vestiges of an "imperial presidency" remain strong in the political culture. This is particularly evident in South Korea's foreign-policy stances.

The Geopolitical Reality

In the U.S., the shock of [the terrorist attacks of] Sept. 11 brought geopolitical concerns into the consciousness of voters, but in Korea these have always been an integral part of every citizen's life. In part this is due to the realities of having survived a fratricidal war that killed more than one million Koreans a half century ago. The possibility of that conflict being reignited at a moment's notice is a very palpable and real threat, given the tenuous armistice agreement.

The Truest Test of Democracy

Democracy is an evolutionary process and there is no one-shoe-fits-all approach to how it should be adopted. No nation can claim to have a perfect democratic system. The truest test is of freedom: that people can openly express their views, choose their leaders and go about their lives without fear or prejudice. This is certainly the case for South Koreans.

South China Morning Post, January 10, 2007.

But on a deeper level, Koreans' internalization of developments outside their border predates the tragic division of the peninsula, and is a function of geopolitical realities. As a relatively small power sandwiched amidst great regional powers for centuries—the "shrimp among whales"—Korea's fate has more often than not been dictated by foreign influences. Thus, it is only natural that Koreans tend to think of Korean national interests in the context of peninsular implications, and then regional developments. Only after that do they think about the global context.

However, in the U.S. strategic thinking tends to follow the opposite course. Americans tend to first think about national interests in relation to the global environment. Then the focus narrows to the regional context, such as Northeast Asia, and only then onto the specific, such as peninsular matters. This is also natural, given America's position in the world and its relative power.

Skewed Strategic Views

For the last half century, while the U.S.-R.O.K. [Republic of Korea] security alliance prevailed as the primary deterrent to the North Korean threat, the pairing of such skewed strategic views posed few problems. In fact, it was the basis for an efficient division of labor between the two allies. However, as South Korea's relative position on the peninsula, the region and the globe has dramatically changed, so too have the expectations of its people and government.

Despite the ongoing menace of North Korea's military threat, South Korea's dominance over the North, according to all economic and social standards, is undeniable: As the world's tenth largest economy, the R.O.K. dwarfs the North; its population is 44 million compared to the North's 22 million; its GDP per capita of over $15,000 is far ahead of the North's $250. South Korea is considered one of the most globalized countries in the world with an economy dependent on international trade, while the North is one of the most closed societies.

By all accounts, the strength of the U.S.-R.O.K. alliance for the last 50 years has allowed the South to prevail in its competition for survival against the North. Yet the alliance is deeply troubled, and its future existence is at a crossroads. One of the primary reasons is precisely the fundamental difference in strategic preferences between South Korea and the U.S.

South Koreans see confrontation with the North as something to be avoided at almost any cost—lest it destroy their hardworn prosperity and freedom. Thus from the South's perspective, the only way to address the North Korean threat is to coax the regime out of isolation and ease its transition into the international community. In the U.S., this type of engagement is criticized as naive at best, and appeasement at worst.

This diametrically opposed view of North Korean threat stems from conflicting perceptions about its source. For the U.S., the "threat" emanates from the traditional sources of the regime's strength, a view that has remained unwavering since the Korean War: its continuation of a military-first policy, including the diversion of scarce national resources into maintaining its million man army; its aggressive missile and nuclear programs; its illicit activities, including counterfeiting; and even its human-rights abuses, which are all signs of the regime's power.

The North Korean Threat

But for South Korea, the "North Korean threat" today emanates not from that regime's strength but rather its weakness: the failure of the economy, the instability of Kim Jong Il's rule and the fragile social conditions. Even illicit activities are considered desperate acts undertaken by a regime struggling to survive. Thus, the real threat posed by North Korea is that the inherently weak system might precipitously collapse, either through an implosion or an explosion that would unleash exorbitant costs on the South. As such, the policy implications are clear: For South Korea, engagement may be unpalatable but it is the only choice, while for the U.S. North Korea's continued threat must be contained.

Arguably, the basis of any alliance is the shared conception of common threats, as had been the basis of the formation of the U.S.-R.O.K. alliance a half-century ago. Today, the threat remains, although the nature of that threat has dramatically changed. Nevertheless, there is no reason that the two countries cannot remain allies, nor does it mean that a common policy cannot be forged.

However, the challenges of doing so have dramatically increased as a function of South Korea's democratization. Ironically, as South Korea has become "freer," the diversity of views over controversial issues such as how to resolve North Korea's nuclear threat has grown. The opportunities to voice opposition have also expanded, allowing for pro-North Korean views to be legitimized. The ultimate paradox of South Korea's democratization maybe that it has benefited the tyrannical North Korean regime.

Despite the seemingly clear results of the Korean elections, it remains unclear whether the Roh Moo Hyun government and the Uri party will alter domestic or foreign policies. Only days after the election, President Roh stated that he would "do [his] best to faithfully carry out the policies the government has started."

The cacophony of clashing opinions and public debate may be a positive development for the South, but the irony is that such freedoms, encouraged and supported by the U.S. for the last half-century, have actually allowed the two Koreas to draw closer together, creating increased Korean resentment of perceived U.S. interference in inter-Korean affairs. Thus, the challenge will be for both South Korean and American political leaders to encourage responsible outcomes that serve the interests not just of Korea but the entire region. Ultimately, the U.S and South Korea share fundamental goals on the Peninsula; the promotion of peaceful reconciliation between the two Koreas that contributes to stability and growth.

> "South Korea's National Assembly has demonstrated the frightful weakness of the county's purported constitutional democracy and has dealt that already frail system another grave blow."

South Korean Democracy Is Threatened

Nicholas Eberstadt

The March 2004 impeachment of South Korean president Roh Mu Hyun, a ploy by opposition parties to gain political advantage, reflects the weakness of South Korea's democracy, argues Nicholas Eberstadt in the following viewpoint. South Korea has struggled with democracy since its inception in 1948, he maintains. Indeed, one former South Korean administration attempted to silence the media and another bribed North Korea to come to a peace agreement, Eberstadt claims. Even if the Constitutional Court overturns Roh's impeachment [which it did in May 2004], the author argues, the South Korean public trust has been violated. Eberstadt is a policy analyst with the conservative American Enterprise Institute.

Nicholas Eberstadt, "A Republic—If South Koreans Can Keep It," *American Enterprise Institute: On the Issues*, April 2004. Copyright 2004 American Enterprise Institute for Public Policy Research. Reproduced with permission of *The American Enterprise*, a national magazine of politics, business, and culture (TAEmag.com).

As you read, consider the following questions:

1. In Eberstadt's opinion, why are South Koreans not famously successful at "keeping" their republics?

2. According to the author, why was Roh Mu Hyun's triumph in the December 2002 presidential election a testimony to the weakness of South Korean democracy?

3. In the author's opinion, what will the South's democratic travails reinforce?

"A republic—if you can keep it." That was Benjamin Franklin's response to an inquiry, at the end of the 1787 Constitutional Convention, about the type of government the founders of the United States had just created. The remark is usually cited as an example of his renowned wit— but Dr. Franklin's comment was deadly serious. He understood that the experiment in constitutional governance is a delicate thing, difficult to maintain and easy to destroy. So we are reminded once again today, as we observe the sad and tawdry constitutional crisis that has suddenly engulfed South Korea with the March 12 [2004] impeachment of President Roh Mu Hyun.[1]

South Korea's foreign allies, including the U.S. government, are bravely pretending that the impeachment drama now underway in Seoul is unexceptional—perhaps even proof of South Korea's "strong, vibrant democracy." Let's not kid ourselves. In voting to strip President Roh of power immediately and to instruct the country's Constitutional Court to determine Roh's final political fate, South Korea's National Assembly has demonstrated the frightful weakness of the country's purported constitutional democracy and has dealt that already frail system another grave blow, from which it is not yet clear it can recover. . . .

1. Roh was elected to a five-year term in February 2003. On March 12, 2004, he was impeached for illegal electioneering, and his own Uri Party soundly defeated the opposition parties (including the Grand National Party) in elections the following month. The impeachment was then overturned in May by the Korean Constitutional Court, which ruled the infraction was too minor to warrant impeachment, and Roh remained in power.

A History of Failure

South Koreans have not been famously successful at "keeping" their republics. They have had *six* of them since the formal establishment of the modern South Korean state in 1948, and they are currently living under a Republic of Korea Constitution that is in its *ninth* version. And yet many Koreans and foreign observers had hoped that the demons that possessed the South Korean body politic were finally exorcised back in 1987, when the country held the first reasonably open and competitive presidential election in the history of the Korean peninsula, heralding a transition from *de facto* military rule to a framework of constitutional democracy.

The three subsequent presidential elections seemed to substantiate those hopes. The victor of the 1992 contest, Kim Young Sam, had been a lifelong civilian politician, not a military surrogate. The 1997 elections went to Kim Dae-jung, a lifelong dissident politician. And the 2002 elections led to the inauguration of Roh Mu Hyun, a human-rights lawyer and outspoken critic of the "old style" of South Korean cronyism.

Signs of Weakness

But the spectacle of Roh's impeachment puts paid to any notion that South Korea's constitutional democracy has grown sturdy and unshakeable roots. The National Assembly is dominated by two opposition parties that loathe the current occupant of the Blue House [the presidential residence of South Korea], and they voted to suspend the country's elected president from his job on the flimsiest of pretexts. Officially, the offenses for which Roh is to be tried—and for which he is already being punished—are some otherwise innocuous comments about the upcoming April 15, [2004,] National Assembly elections. Roh, who had renounced his membership of the ruling Millennium Democratic Party [in the fall of 2003], let it be known that he hoped candidates from the Uri Party would do well, and he thought he might eventually join that organization.

The Politics of the Chosun Dynasty

Politics in Korea's last monarchy, the Chosun dynasty (1392–1910), was a vicious "winner-take-all" affair. The losers faced confiscation of their property, exile, and often execution. In a Confucian culture that elevated the rule of men over the rule of law, everything was permissible for those in power. Further, the sins of the fathers were not only visited on the children but on the grandchildren as well, as three generations of family members were enslaved or exterminated. Unfortunately, in spite of the glib rhetoric about South Korea's "vibrant democracy" in the Western media, South Korean politics today resemble the politics of the Chosun dynasty.

Won Joon Choe, Asia Times,
September 4, 2004.

Lawmakers were shocked—shocked!—that the president would dare sully the nation's pristine electoral process through such nefarious interference. Their reading of the law held Roh's words to be a violation of election rules preventing the president from using the power of his office to influence parliamentary contests. The ploy was utterly transparent, but the written constitution gave them all the authority they needed to proceed with the motion.

The truth is that the impeachment had nothing to do with the rule of law. The country's National Election Commission had already ruled Roh's faux pas to be a minor one. However, what the National Assembly provided was a perfect model of "rule *by* law"—the opportunistic, unprincipled, and entirely situational use of formal legal statutes by the powerful to gain political advantage. Such a practice has been the bane of unscrupulous Confucian governments throughout East Asian history.

The Misuse of Right and Responsibility

With this patent misuse of its important right and responsibility, the National Assembly has exposed the weakness in contemporary South Korean democracy. If you or I learned that a beloved friend or relative had been found wandering naked in the street, our first reaction would probably be horror—but then we might think back and recognize that there had been warning signs of the impending breakdown. So it is with South Korea's democratic system: gathering signs of trouble were there, whether or not we cared to take them seriously.

We might now remember how President Kim Dae-jung—that avowed champion of openness, law, and democracy—launched tax probes against local media, a move many saw as an attempt to intimidate publications that criticized his policies. (In 1999, the International Press Institute in Vienna even sent the future Nobel Laureate a letter begging him to desist from his campaign against South Korea's free press—a missive that was all but ignored internationally.) Then there was the acclaimed Kim Dae-jung/Kim Jong Il summit in Pyong-yang [North Korea's capital] in June 2000—the supposedly historic "peace break-through" that later turned out to have been purchased furtively and illegally, with a price tag of at least $100 million, through the transfer of South Korean taxpayer money to the "Dear Leader's" bank accounts in Macau.

Roh Mu Hyun's triumph in the December 2002 presidential plebiscite was itself testimony to the weakness of South Korean democracy. His main selling point was not his allergy to the United States (genuine as that may be), but rather his outsider's resume: his manifest lack of experience in Seoul's payola-driven politics, a system that the great majority of voters already viewed with distrust and disdain.

Once in office, Roh's amateurish and inconstant performance, as well as his own cynical attempts to game the system, did little to allay popular misgivings about the health of

149

South Korean democracy. Recall that after barely eight months in office, a frustrated and tactically outclassed President Roh toyed with pulling a coup d'état *against himself* by demanding an extra-constitutional referendum to back his policies and threatening to resign from the presidency if the vote did not turn out to his liking. In the event, Roh himself quickly dropped the idea of exiting from office before his term was up, but as the impeachment attests, his enemies did not follow suit.

Playing into Our Dear Leader's Hands

Now the impeachment process must grind forward, and from the standpoint of the endangered democratic system, none of the possible outcomes are reassuring. On the one hand, the court may rule that Roh has violated his oath of office and must quit the presidency—in which case a scandalously low threshold for rejecting the legitimacy of the people's highest elected representative will have been established and ratified for all future South Korean leaders. On the other hand, the court may let Roh keep his job. Then the public will be forced to choose between a president they know to be too small for his office and a National Assembly they know they cannot trust.

There is, of course, a winner in this unfolding tragedy. His name is Kim Jong II. With South Korea in political turmoil, North Korea's degree of freedom in its nuclear confrontation with the Western world expands quite nicely. In the immediate future, the DPRK [Democratic People's Republic of Korea] need no longer worry about coordinated international efforts to press Pyongyang for nuclear compliance, because those efforts would inevitably require coordination with the now-dysfunctional government in Seoul.

Over the longer term, the South's current travails will only reinforce the North's appetite for an unconditional Korean re-unification—on the North's terms. For nearly six decades,

North Korean doctrine has maintained that the South Korean political system is riddled with rot, tottering under its own contradictions, and ready for a fall. That propaganda sounds uncomfortably plausible today.

For their own sake—and the world's—South Koreans must prove Kim Jong II wrong. It is their republic—if they can keep it.

> "[North Korean prisoners] were worked to death in mines or building secret tunnels for the military, or given lethal jobs like testing chemical weapons."

North Korea Violates the Human Rights of Its People

Jasper Becker

In the following viewpoint Jasper Becker maintains that the North Korean regime of Kim Jong-Il violates the human rights of millions of his people. Kim lives in luxury while his people starve, Becker claims. In fact, he alleges, the North Korean regime kept for itself U.N. aid intended to feed starving North Koreans. Trainloads of those suspected of disloyalty are sent to camps without trial, and political prisoners are abused and killed for little reason, Becker contends. Becker is author of Rogue Regime: Kim Jon Il and the Looming Threat of North Korea.

As you read, consider the following questions:

1. According to Becker, how does China deal with North Koreans who escape to China?
2. In the author's view, why does Kim have a crack force similar to Saddam Hussein's Republican Guard?

Jasper Becker, "A Gulag with Nukes: Inside North Korea," *Open Democracy*, July 19, 2005. Reproduced by permission.

3. In the author's opinion, how has the United Nations led the way toward absolving Kim of responsibility for his crimes against humanity?

The Chinese shopkeeper gave a triumphant yell when he spotted a ragged figure bent double and stumbling about the garbage that had cascaded from a hilltop. I plunged after him through the deep snow. When I caught up with him, he was shouting and grinning at his successful catch.

As he fished around his pocket to pull out some plastic twine, a face black with dirt and scabrous with pellagra shrunk back into the shadows of a hood made from grey sackcloth like a medieval leper. The creature whimpered feebly but put up no resistance as the shopkeeper bound the twine around her hands. I now found myself bargaining for the life of a woman I guessed to be around 50.

She turned out to be 28. She had been a worker in Hamhung, North Korea's second largest industrial city. All the factories had closed. Her husband had disappeared and she was left with no rations to try to look after her 5-year old. "Without work, you get no food", she said.

A Slave Society

After some haggling, I managed to buy her life for 200 *yuan* (around #13 or $20). This was 1997, at the height of the North Korean famine when 3 million out of 22 million perished in (proportionately) the worst man-made famine ever recorded in peacetime. To call her or the hundreds of thousands like her "refugees" is a misnomer; they are escapees from the last slave society left in the world.

Eight years on, the North Koreans are still starving and the west still does not know how to deal with their "dear leader", Kim Jong-Il—who inherited the state leadership from his father, "great leader" Kim Il-sung, in 1994. Washington's elite remains deeply divided about whether it is wiser to appease or confront him.

Kim has agreed to return to the six-party nuclear talks (involving Russia, China, Japan, North Korea, South Korea and the United States) he abandoned; the talks resume[d] in Beijing [China] on 26 July 2005.

At the last showdown in 2002, the Bush administration put its trust in China, which in turn promised to force North Korea to the negotiating table and make it give up its nuclear weapons. China has let Bush down, and for a very clear reason—it is part of the problem. Every year, China forcibly sends back across the border 25,000 North Korean escapees, many of whom are then shot or imprisoned in death camps.

China claims they are all "economic migrants" and forbids the United Nations High Commission for Refugees from opening camps and processing claims for political asylum. China is determined to prevent its vassal from collapsing, East Germany-style; its support for North Korea is part of a pattern that has seen it give uncritical support to regimes like Pol Pot's Cambodia and, more recently, the Darfur-oppressing Islamist junta in Sudan and Islam Karimov's Uzbekistan.

The Court of Kim Jong-Il

When, one day, the Kim Jong-Il regime falls and the mass graves open up in North Korea, the United Nations will get the blame. The World Food Programme has run the largest and longest emergency food programme in its history. It boasts that it averted a great famine in the late 1990s, and that by careful monitoring, it is now protecting the neediest members of society.

The trouble is that when North Koreans are free to speak, they tell a very different story. In Seoul [North Korea's capital] in June 2005, I met Choi Seung-cheol, who saw thousands of emaciated bodies arriving at the hospital in Chongjin where he worked as a doctor. This industrial port on the east coast was one of the first to receive international aid, but he reckoned that over 200,000 died there. At the hospital, they worked without any medical supplies because 90% of the foreign aid was confiscated.

"They kept everything for themselves", he said. He and many others I interviewed believe that billions of dollars in foreign aid has been diverted, partly to fund the northern state's weapons programmes and partly to finance Kim Jong-Il's luxurious daily routine.

South Korea's defence ministry estimates that Kim spent $400 million in 1997–2002 buying second-hand MiG fighter jets, submarine parts, helicopters, and engines for tanks and ships. His troops are equipped with mini-underwater submarines launched from disguised fishing vessels, specially adapted hovercrafts, light planes and a defence industry hidden inside mountains which builds ballistic missiles, nuclear weapons and chemical gases in subterranean factories and research laboratories.

The costliest part of it all is the nuclear-weapons programmes, much of which Kim has probably been able to hide as effectively as the Iranians have hidden theirs from United Nations inspectors. This is in addition to an intercontinental ballistic missile programme whose scope caught every one by surprise on 31 August 1998 when Kim fired a rocket which flew over Japan.

An Extravagant Lifestyle

The stories told about the extravagance of Kim Jong-Il's lifestyle are so lurid that at first they seem hard to believe. A number of former cooks, including an Italian and a Japanese sushi chef, have described in detail his gourmet obsessions. One chef published a book in Japan under the pseudonym Kenji Fujimoto; at the very time people were starving in their millions, he travelled to Iran and Uzbekistan to buy caviar, to China for melons and grapes, to Thailand and Malaysia for durians and papayas, to the Czech Republic for Pilsner beer, to Denmark for bacon, and (regularly) to Japan for tuna and other fresh fish.

© 2006 John Trever, *Albuquerque Journal*

When I tracked down a member of one of Kim's "happiness teams" of dancers and masseuses in Seoul, I asked her if these tales could be true. O Yong-hui, a petite slender woman with a pale porcelain complexion and almond eyes started out as a professional gymnast until she was recruited to join one of the four all-girl dance troupes. She is now 33.

She described how, on joining Kim's court, she was given handmade Italian shoes, Japanese designer clothes (Yamoto, Kenzo, Mori) and an Omega watch inscribed with Kim Jong-Il's name. A check of Swiss trade statistics shows that in 1998, North Korea did indeed import $2.7 million's worth of luxury watches.

At breakfast she enjoyed French croissants, fresh yoghurt and imported fruits because Kim said they must have clear and healthy skins. At lunch there was fresh raw fish, Japanese-style, and at dinner Korean or western dishes.

"We ate off porcelain dishes inlaid with roses and used silver tableware. Everything was imported. Nothing I have ever seen in South Korea is as good", she said. When her five years was up—no girls stay longer—she decided to flee with her husband, a former bodyguard.

I double-checked their stories with an ex-bodyguard, Lee Young-guk who observed Kim at close quarters during eleven years of service.

"In a real sense, he is the richest man in the world. There are no limits on what he can do", Lee said. "He has at least ten palaces set in sprawling grounds and insists each is always occupied by thousands of staff so his enemies are never sure where he is. They contain golf courses, stables for his horses, garages full of motor-bikes and luxury cars, shooting-ranges, swimming pools, cinemas, funfair parks, water-jet bikes and hunting grounds stocked with wild deer and duck."

A big bulky man in a blue suit, Lee reached down below the coffee table, and showed me shins covered by a mass of blue scars. When Lee Young-guk returned to his home to find everyone starving, he decided to escape; but North Korean agents masquerading as South Koreans caught him in China. His strong physique and years of harsh training helped him survive the torture, and he escaped again.

Lee says that Kim Jong-Il fears an uprising like the one that overthrew Nicolae Ceausescu in Romania. In the face of several abortive army rebellions, he relies on a crack force of around 100,000 men, the equivalent of Saddam Hussein's Republican Guard.

After the Soviet bloc's collapse and the defeat of Saddam Hussein in the first Gulf war of 1991, Kim took ever-greater internal security measures. He expanded the secret police, creating three duplicate layers of surveillance. No one in the elite could go anywhere or meet anyone without first obtaining his permission.

After the United States tried to "decapitate" Saddam Hussein in the second Iraq war of 2003, he disappeared for four months and moved around Pyongyang [North Korea's capital] using a series of tunnels that connect all key buildings and were designed to withstand a nuclear attack.

A Gulag with Nukes

When Madeleine Albright, then US secretary of state, travelled to Pyongyang to meet Kim in 2000 and arrange a summit with President [Bill] Clinton, she was told he was reclusive, even delusional—a weak, cautious man hampered by a stammer who lived in the shadow of his father Kim Il-Sung. She found instead, she reported, a charming if eccentric man who seemed reassuringly rational.

If indeed Washington can do business with Kim Jong-Il, he would first have to be absolved from any responsibility for his crimes against humanity. The United Nations, anxious to continue operating in the north, has led the way by officially blaming "temporary" food shortages on bad weather and the loss of Soviet aid after 1990.

But you only have to meet North Koreans to see compelling evidence of malnutrition that began twenty years ago. I met kids on the border who claimed to be 19 or 22; they had the physiques of 10-year-olds.

Lee Min-bok is a refugee in Seoul, an agricultural expert. Kim Jong-Il told his father in 1982 that the country had reaped a record harvest of fifteen million tons of grain—double the true figure. Under Kim Jong-Il, lying became so endemic that it destroyed the planned economy.

Everyone learned how to please the "dear leader"; all you had to do was lie. People started to cheat by making false reports. By the mid-1980s, the country was running short of a million tons of grain every year, enough to feed 3 million people. Lee Min-bok first saw people dying of hunger in 1988, in North Korea's north-east, seven years before the country appealed for international aid.

Lee Min-bok's research proved that the country could feed itself if it embraced Chinese-style agricultural reforms. Kim Jong-Il refused to consider any reform and Lee, fearing for his life, decided to flee.

The Fate of Doubters

Those who doubt (or are even suspected of doubting) Kim's fantasy world are sent to places like Camp 22. Ahn Myong-chol, now a banker in Seoul, spent a decade working as a guard in various camps. He can still recall the shock—"like a hammer"—on first seeing dwarf-like creatures milling about in filthy rags.

"They were walking skeletons of skin and bone, with faces covered in cuts and scars where they had been beaten. Most had no ears; they had been torn off in beatings. Many had lost a leg and hobbled about on crude crutches or sticks", Ahn remembers.

Ahn was told not to consider the prisoners human beings. They were killed casually for the slightest infractions, often in gruesome ways—buried alive, dragged behind jeeps, hung or shot, garrotted or burned alive. The rest were worked to death in mines or building secret tunnels for the military, or given lethal jobs like testing chemical weapons.

"Anyone suspected of disloyalty ended up in the camps", he said. Kim Il-sung had purged opponents by the trainload, but his son nearly doubled the number of political prisoners. Whole families would be arrested, and sent to prison camps without trial and without even knowing their crime.

Kang Chol-hwan describes his camp childhood in his book *The Aquariums of Pyongyang*. When President Bush invited him to the White House, Pyongyang reacted furiously, calling Kang "human trash" and threatening the United States with a refusal to consider further talks if it continued to "insult" North Korea.

The *New York Times* and the rest of liberal America wants Bush to start serious negotiations and stop calling Kim Jong-Il names. President Bush is certain to ignore this advice. As the Beijing six-party talks prepare to reconvene on 26 July, the stage is set for a new showdown on the Korean peninsula.

> "North Korea itself . . . must decide how
> to create a system of rules that protects
> human rights."

North Korea Should Be Encouraged to Develop Its Own Human Rights Reforms

John Feffer

Rather than isolate and punish North Korea for its human rights abuses, governments and human rights organizations should encourage North Korea to develop its own human rights program, claims John Feffer in the following viewpoint. The North Korean government should be given access to human rights assistance in the same way it is given economic and technical assistance, he maintains. According to Feffer, helping North Korea create its own human rights reforms as part of the international community will be more successful than imposing human rights reforms on the nation. Feffer is author of North Korea/South: U.S. Policy at a Time of Crisis.

As you read, consider the following questions:

1. In Feffer's view, what has been the defect in U.S. policy on North Korean human rights abuses?

John Feffer, "Human Rights in North Korea and the U.S. Strategy of Linkage," *Znet*, January 15, 2006. Reproduced by permission.

2. What is the problem with the mind-set that human rights and the nuclear impasse should be linked, according to the author?

3. In the author's opinion, what are the drawbacks of a heterogeneous approach to human rights?

Though it would be difficult to find anyone in the United States who would praise North Korea for its dismal human rights record, this consensus by no means extends to practical foreign policy. In other words, there is broad agreement on what is wrong in North Korea, from the political labor camps to the lack of basic freedoms of speech and assembly, but little agreement on what to do about it or who should be doing it.

Linking Human Rights and the Nuclear Crisis

At the governmental level, policymakers are divided on whether to link the human rights issue to other pressing concerns such as the nuclear crisis or humanitarian aid. In Congress, an effort is under way to build on existing legislation and embed the human rights movement in a grand "regime change" strategy targeting the world's remaining dictatorships, but financial considerations and traditional balance-of-power calculations may derail this initiative. In the world of nongovernmental organizations (NGOs), an evangelical movement has clothed its primary concern for religious freedom in the garb of universal human rights and has gained much political capital, thanks to vocal church support and a faith-based climate of opinion. But mainstream human rights organizations—as well as mainstream. religious organizations such as the National Council of Churches—remain wary of the missionary zeal and hard-line strategies of these evangelicals.

Divergent strategic approaches might suggest a diversity of policy alternatives on the issue of North Korean human rights, but the discussion taking place in the United States is rather narrow. Indeed, one of the grave defects of U.S. policy on this issue, from the governmental level to the NGO level, has been its myopia. Given the human rights record of the Bush administration and its predilection for using the human rights records of other countries as a justification for regime change, it may well be impossible for the United States to devise a more nuanced and effective human rights policy toward North Korea. . . .

The policy debate in the United States, and particularly in Washington, has largely focused on whether to link human rights to the current nuclear impasse—either in a genuine effort to improve human rights in North Korea or to force regime change—or to delink the two and proceed with dispatch to settle the nuclear question. The narrowness of this agenda is partly a legacy of the 1970s, when a similar question influenced the fate of U.S.-Soviet détente. This mind-set stems in part from the demands of policymaking in Washington, which boils down to amendments to legislation and ways to affect the appropriations process. It also derives from the hard-line NGO coalition of neoconservatives and evangelicals for whom the strategy of linkage offers a perfect convergence of interests. . . .

The Perils of Linkage

The perils of linkage include disrupting current negotiations over the nuclear issue and threatening the overall engagement strategy—much as linkage unraveled U.S.-Soviet détente in the 1970s. The focus on whether to link or not to link has also obscured other approaches to human rights questions connected to North Korea, though these blueprints are not without their own drawbacks. North Korea might view the basket approach as a soft regime change strategy; quiet diplomatic efforts require patience and a long-term perspective, and the lack of media attention does little to advertise the benefits of this plan; the expanded definition of human rights doesn't paint North Korea in any better colors and neglects the political and civil dimension of the current economic crisis; and economic engagement carries with it the whiff of a "poisoned carrot" and the probability of political crackdowns a la Singapore or China, as the North Korean leadership attempts to restrict reform from expanding beyond the economic sector.

Despite (or perhaps because of) the above defects, these policy alternatives suggest that a heterogeneous approach stands the greatest chance of success—if success is measured by a general improvement in the economic well-being of the population and a reduction in the most egregious human rights violations such as summary executions and political labor camps. South Korea, Japan, Europe, and the United States are always going to view North Korea differently, given their distinctive ethnic and geopolitical lenses of interpretation. It might be appropriate, therefore, that these varied actors take on separate roles: Europe pursuing quiet diplomacy, South Korea engaging the North economically, humanitarian NGOs focusing on food as a human right, and the U.S. government along with mainstream human rights NGOs undertaking "name and shame" activities.

The Drawbacks of a Heterogeneous Approach

There are, however, two drawbacks to this approach of functional diversity. "Name and shame" activities are a vital component of human rights work, whether applied to North Korea's labor camps or U.S. detention facilities in Iraq and Cuba. But "name and shame" activities, if promoted by a powerful actor like the U.S. government, can overwhelm all the other strategies, making South Korea's engagement policy, for instance, weaker internationally and more scorned domestically. It is important, therefore, to strive for some measure of balance among the different strategies. It is also important to acknowledge that different actors within countries pursue a variety of strategies. In the United States, the State Department has shown some support for the "bundling" approach, while several U.S. NGOs are engaged in quiet diplomacy— even as key figures in the Bush administration have concentrated on shaming Pyongyang.

The second drawback is perhaps more fundamental. Not all organizations working on human rights in North Korea share the same goals. During the era of the Helsinki Accords, even the most vocal human rights organizations in the Soviet bloc didn't call for the collapse of their governments. Efforts were directed toward improving human rights within the current systems. Today, however, several of the more vocal human rights organizations—both neoconservative and evangelical— have the maximalist agenda of erasing North Korea from the map. In the 1970s, neoconservatives devised linkage to undercut détente; today, the linkage problem relates not simply to the viability of engagement but to the very survival of the North Korean state. To the extent that human rights activities are linked to government collapse, they risk creating greater human rights problems than they purport to solve. While these potential problems—including economic crisis, refugee outflow, violent factional disputes, loose nukes, and even war—are of obvious concern to the international community, they pose the greatest threat to Koreans themselves. South Korea already faces challenges assimilating several thousands North Korean defectors: tens of thousands would overwhelm the system. The great disparity between the two economies— much larger than that between East and West Germany in 1989—suggests that sudden economic integration would send South Korea into a prolonged crisis. Even collapse without integration would jeopardize the south's economic standing (not to mention the impact on northeast China, home to thousands of ethnic Koreans). It is no surprise, then, that except for a fringe element, Korean politicians and social movements seek to avoid regime collapse in the North.

An Internal Solution

If the scenario of functional diversity is to succeed, it must be clearly distinguished from state-elimination agendas. Governments and organizations should commit to an improvement of the political and economic welfare of North Koreans within their existing system, however modified that system might become. Human rights should be viewed as part of the engagement strategy, not contrary to it. Moreover, this engagement approach, which has largely been restricted to North-South relations, must be embedded in a much larger process of integration.

The first step in a diversified game plan involves the Northeast Asian community. China has proposed institutionalizing the Six-Party Talks, which would give the region its first multilateral security forum. A chief virtue of institutionalizing the Six-Party Talks is that North Korea would become a working member of the East Asian community. Ideally, these regional discussions would expand beyond the nuclear issue to include economic cooperation and the human dimension. To be effective, such an approach should adopt an expanded definition of human rights, should avoid any direct references to the civil society experiences of the Helsinki Accords, and should borrow from the experience of quiet diplomacy in offering North Korean government officials access to the same kind of technical assistance in the human rights realm that they've been given in the economic and legal sector. Moreover, at least at first, China can play a key role in articulating a human rights formula that can elicit North Korean cooperation, perhaps under the general rubric of "human security" and in the context of a working group established within the Six-Party Talks. Such a "human security" framework might emphasize social and economic rights and only gradually address political and civil questions. Improving human rights in North Korea to China's level, while not ideal, is at least a pragmatic goal, and North Korea is certainly more likely on this issue to listen to the experiences of Chinese leaders than to the advice of American or Japanese officials.

Integrating into the International Community

But regional integration is only the first step in harmonizing North Korea's human rights policies with global norms. To meet international standards, North Korea must be ushered further into the international community. Such integration is the most effective path through which economic, political, and social benefits can flow to North Korea. By the same token, for a coercive policy to work with North Korea—from mild censure to more extreme cancellation of programs—the country must have a greater stake in the worldwide family of nations. Pyongyang must perceive that it has something to lose if it doesn't conform to global expectations, and North Korea must be sufficiently in the public eye that its reputation becomes a factor in its calculations.

Both "name and shame" activists and engagement advocates should keep this integration framework in mind when pursuing their very different, but at times complementary, agendas. But they should avoid viewing themselves in simply a good cop, bad cop, carrot, or stick role. North Korea must be seen as a subject and not just an object. Ultimately North Korea itself, either the leadership or the citizenry but ideally both, must decide how to create a system of rules that protects human rights. Outside actors should think in terms of providing the tools with which North Koreans can erect a human rights infrastructure themselves rather than simply pursuing a "carrot and stick" approach that pushes North Korea like an unthinking mule toward a destination that only a supposedly wiser rider can see.

> "[South Korean] engagement without even the strings of human decency attached serves only to persuade the North's Kim Jong-Il that he can get away with anything."

South Korea Should Not Ignore Human Rights Violations in North Korea

Economist

South Korea's unconditional engagement without demands that the North improve its human rights record hurts the South's reputation in the international community, claim the editors of the Economist, *a British newsmagazine. In the following viewpoint the authors add that the South's failure to cooperate with human rights organizations trying to help North Korean political refugees further adds to the perception that it does not care about fellow Koreans suffering in the North. Since turning a blind eye has won no concessions, the authors argue, the South should hold the North more accountable.*

As you read, consider the following questions:

1. According to the *Economist*, why is it not easy living next door to North Korea?

2. In the authors' opinion, about what shameful situation has South Korea kept quiet?

3. How does China deal with North Korean refugees who flee across its borders, in the authors' view?

A Shameful Policy and Nothing to Show for It

It isn't easy living next door to hard-faced North Korea. Even before it took to brandishing its "nuclear deterrent" at all comers, South Koreans were living in the sights of thousands of artillery guns and missiles that could rain all-too-conventional destruction on their cities. In hopes of better relations, . . . , South Korean governments have promoted engagement over confrontation with the prickly North. Demands for "reciprocity"—better behaviour—from North Korea have also been set aside. Such no-strings engagement has its costs. Right now it is making life that bit harder for vulnerable North Koreans hoping to flee political repression at home and make their way via China and places like Cambodia, Laos, Mongolia, Myanmar, Vietnam and Russia to seek asylum in the South.

The NGOs [nongovernmental organizations] and missionaries working along the Chinese border with North Korea are used to having no support from the South Korean government, which perennially fears that if the refugee trickle (fewer than 2,000 North Koreans reached South Korea [in 2004], up from a handful in the early 1990s) becomes a flood, North Korea may lash out—or collapse and become a costly burden. Shamefully, South Korea also keeps quiet about close to 500 of its citizens thought to have been abducted over the years by North Korean agents.

A Betrayal of the Korean People

The United Nations General Assembly voted on a resolution condemning the violation of human rights in North Korea [on November 17, 2005]. Eighty-four nations stood on the side of principle and voted to condemn the Pyongyang regime's "widespread human rights violations, including torture, public executions, arbitrary detention, the absence of due process, the imposition of the death penalty for political reasons, the large number of prison camps and the extensive use of forced labor." . . .

All the while, South Korea, the presumptive sole legitimate government on the Korean peninsula, with the world as its stage, chose to stand in the wings and avert its gaze. Never a laggard when it comes to stressing common ethnic ties with the people of the North, South Korea nonetheless joined the 62 apathetic or fence-straddling nations . . . and abstained.

Sung-Yoon Lee, Weekly Standard, *January 23, 2006.*

Now South Korea's unification minister has in effect said sorry to North Korea for the embarrassment caused [in July 2004] when 468 refugees who had fetched up in Vietnam were flown to the South: there will be no more such large-scale rescues, he said. There is talk too of making travel harder for those (admittedly a few of them profiteers, but most of them not) who help North Koreans escape.

The refugees already have a hard time of it. At home, those deemed hostile to the regime (or not supportive enough) receive less food. Up to 200,000 political prisoners are held in labour camps; their families down to three generations are often treated similarly harshly. A few manage to flee over the border into China. But despite having signed international conventions governing protection of refugees, China hunts them out, brands them "criminals" and dumps them back in North Korea where punishment awaits.

Bad Form, but Bad Policy Too

South Korea generously takes in those North Koreans who do make it—around 5,000 so far. But there are good reasons for holding North Korea, and China, more accountable over human-rights abuses and the mistreatment of refugees. One is that the scandal over such abuses is set to grow. The UN [in 2004] appointed a special rapporteur to look at human rights in North Korea. America is soon to appoint a special envoy too. As more stories of the human-rights horrors in the North become known, including through the South's increasingly feisty press and parliament, the South Korean government risks seeing its own reputation tarnished by keeping mum.

Besides, refusing to take up the issue has won no concessions from North Korea. On the contrary, engagement without even the strings of human decency attached serves only to persuade the North's Kim Jong-Il that he can get away with anything, and that he has South Korea's government in his pocket, along with all the food, fertiliser, coal and other goodies it offers. South Korea's government, meanwhile, gets the worst of all worlds: the appearance of acquiescing in the ill-treatment of fellow Koreans, and nothing to show for it.

> *"President [George W.] Bush would do well to insist on making the North Korean human rights problem a priority."*

The United States Should Make North Korean Human Rights a Priority

Sing-Yoon Lee

The United States should take the lead in making the condemnation of North Korea's repressive regime and appalling human rights record an international priority, argues Sing-Yoon Lee in the following viewpoint. The Bush administration made great strides when Bush invited North Korean refugees to the Oval Office to tell their horrific stories, Lee claims. Nevertheless, Lee asserts, the United States should open its doors to more North Korean refugees and put more pressure on South Korea to take a stand against repression in the North. Lee is a research associate at the Korea Institute at Harvard University.

As you read, consider the following questions:

1. According to Lee, whom does South Korea blame for increasing tensions with North Korea?

2. What was the significance of welcoming North Korean refugees for settlement in the United States, according to the author?

3. In the author's opinion, what is the hoped-for result of international attention to the North Korean human rights problem?

Contrary to popular belief, the party left most isolated by the U.N. Security Council's unanimous condemnation of North Korea's missile launches and nuclear programs is not the reclusive Pyongyang [North Korean] regime, but the other Korea, the affluent one south of the 38th parallel. After all, Kim Jong Il—the "general," as his people call him, although he never served in the military—can at least bet on his devoted suitors in the South Korean government to keep making passes at him. Kim's top suitor in Seoul [South Korea's capital], President Roh Moo Hyun, was abandoned not only by his American and Japanese friends—who pointedly shunned South Korea in discussions leading up to the U.N. resolution—but also by the Dear Leader [Kim Jong Il] himself.

The Pressure on South Korea

A week after North Korea's July 4 missile barrage, a barely noticed follow-up tantrum by Kim's visiting envoys shook South Korea to its core. True to its criminal form, the general's delegation wined and dined in Pusan [South Korea] on a ministerial-level date, slapped around their southern suitors, and demanded that they pay up protection money. As a token of appreciation for the magnanimous protection, the general's gang further demanded that their southern protectorate suspend joint military exercises with the United States, abolish its anti-Communist national security law, and make sure to pay respects on their next visit to Pyongyang at the "sacred site" where the Great Leader, the general's late father, reposes embalmed.

When the southern hosts, somewhat stunned, demurred, their northern guests stormed out of the room cursing that South Korea will "pay a price" for the "collapse" of the relationship, and that an "unforeseeable" future now lies ominously before them.

Attacking U.S. Policy

In the days following the seven-rocket salute, the South Korean president, clearly dumbfounded by the general's forwardness, began to point a finger at Japan and the United States for heightening tensions. As for the missiles themselves, the Roh government called them a "mere political gesture." When the media pointed out that all seven missiles had the range to reach any part of South Korea, a high-ranking politician from Roh's party retorted that the missiles were defensive in nature, and even if fired in a southerly direction would only be used to target U.S. forces in Korea. This came after days of insistence by the South Korean government, leading up to the blasts, that the North was planning only a harmless satellite launch.

While the United States, Japan, China, Russia, Britain, and France were brainstorming to come up with the right wording for a rebuke of Pyongyang, President Roh was busy complaining to aides about the U.S. policy of squeezing the North, which he described with an ancient Chinese expression, "strike first, settle later." Roh explained to his less erudite men that an example of such American impetuosity would be the U.S. insistence on "examining North Korea's accounts, without presenting any evidence of that regime's counterfeiting of U.S. dollars." The inference to be drawn by his aides was that Washington was unjustly bullying the general in Pyongyang for harmlessly playing with his missiles. After the Security Council condemned the North on July 15, Roh pleaded for patience: "We must take special note that the creation of a state

The Strength of International Sanctions

As the members of the United Nations Security Council grapple with possible financial and technological sanctions against North Korea in response to its launch of several missiles on [October 9, 2006], they should add another sanction to the debate: a judicial intervention focusing on the catastrophic human rights situation in North Korea.

Kim Jong Il's regime is responsible for crimes against humanity, genocide and war crimes. From 150,000 to 200,000 people are now being held in gulag-like prison camps where they suffer enslavement, torture, rape and near starvation.

One million people are estimated to have died in these camps, adding to the one to two million deaths from the famine caused by government failures in the 1990s.

David Scheffer & Grace Kang,
International Herald Tribune, July 6, 2006.

of needless tension and confrontation by the excessive reaction of certain parties is not conducive to problem-solving."

A Wayward Ally

After such an astonishing performance from Seoul, how should the Bush administration respond to its wayward ally?

One approach would be to treat the unwelcome noises from Seoul as Washington does those emanating from Pyongyang: Ignore them. Forbearance will be rewarded, perhaps in a generation or two. Historians will note that for five years George W. Bush patiently put up with a most unhelpful ally in Roh Moo Hyun's South Korea during a critical period of America's war on terror and campaign against the proliferation of nuclear weapons. No matter what, future generations of Koreans—those who value freedom and democracy—will remain grateful to Bush for what he will have achieved during his eight years in office: containing Kim Jong Il's threat to Koreans in both the North and the South and, perhaps more important, reining in Seoul's unprincipled appeasement of Kim.

Yet there is a better way. President Bush can salvage the once-healthy U.S.-South Korea relationship by engaging the people of South and North Korea. Koreans will come to regard him as they do Harry Truman—as their savior. Just as President Truman saved South Korea in June 1950 by coming to its defense against North Korea's invasion, President Bush should open America's doors more widely to North Korean refugees, thereby saving lives and awakening the South Korean people to the crimes of the Kim Jong Il regime.

Welcoming North Korean Refugees

On May 5 [2006] the United States welcomed ordinary North Korean refugees for resettlement for the first time. It was a major symbolic step in the growing global campaign to raise awareness of the abuses of the totalitarian regime in Pyongyang. It was an act of compassion, courage, and leadership, as it was undertaken despite considerable grumbling from sophisticates in the United States and South Korea. It was, in the simplest sense, an act that could not have taken place had the president of the United States himself not felt compassion for the suffering of the North Korean people.

Coming out of an April 28 [2006] Oval Office meeting with North Korean refugees and the family of a Japanese woman abducted by North Korea when she was 13, President Bush said, "I have just had one of the most moving meetings since I've been the president." The previous June, President Bush had invited to the White House Kang Chol Hwan, the survivor of 10 years in a North Korean concentration camp for political prisoners. In contrast, to public knowledge, President Roh has not yet met a single North Korean refugee, although over 8,000 refugees have made their way into South Korea.

In the aftermath of U.N. Security Council Resolution 1695, the United States will no doubt continue to press South Korea to join the multinational effort to prevent the transit of weapons of mass destruction into and out of the North. South Korea's cooperation will be sought in the ongoing measures against North Korea's money-laundering and counterfeiting. The United States will insist that Seoul keep a watchful eye on transfers of hard currency into the North, which may be used to finance the building and buying of weapons of mass destruction. And Washington will continue to lean on South Korea to stand with global public opinion on North Korea's human rights violations.

However, all indications are that such exhortations will fall on deaf ears. President Roh seems to believe that the only way to salvage his floundering presidency, with an approval rating hovering in the mid-teens, is through a dramatic summit embrace with Kim Jong Il sometime before his term expires in February 2008.

Making Repression an International Issue

At the next meeting between Bush and Roh, whether in Washington or at the Asia-Pacific Economic Cooperation (APEC) meeting in Vietnam in November [2006], President Bush would do well to insist on making the North Korean human rights problem a priority. During Roh's visit to the White House, Bush might even invite a few North Korean refugees so that President Roh will finally have a chance to meet them. By continuing to make Kim Jong Il's systematic repression a high-profile international issue, President Bush would reaffirm to the world and to the Korean people his commitment to address one of the most egregious humanitarian disasters in history. Allowing more North Korean refugees into the United States would be eloquent in its symbolism.

Just as the United States, with Japan's support, took the initiative in galvanizing world opinion on the question of North Korea's missiles, so, too, should the United States take the leadership role in uniting the international community in condemning North Korea's heartless tyranny. President Roh, pining for a meeting with Kim Jong Il during the next year and a half of his term, will protest. But the people of North and South Korea will listen.

With more international attention to the North Korean human rights problem, and with further reports of what the United States is doing for North Korean refugees, South Korea might finally free itself of its insidious infatuation with the general. And George W. Bush will be remembered with gratitude by generations of Koreans for his concern for the people of both the North and South. That's a legacy that would make any American president proud.

Periodical Bibliography

The following articles have been selected to supplement the diverse views presented in this chapter.

America	"North Korea's Other Problem," January 15, 2007.
Elizabeth Goldberg	"Closed Society: Despite a Decade-Long Globalization Push, South Korea's Legal Market Remains a Hermit Kingdom, at Least for Now," *American Lawyer*, October 2006.
Andrei Lankov	"Bitter Taste of Paradise: North Korean Refugees in South Korea," *Journal of East Asian Studies*, January–April 2006.
B.J. Lee	"South Korea: Too Much Activism? The Country's Idealistic '386 Generation' Helped Usher in Democracy, but Has Bungled Its Political Opportunity," *Newsweek*, November 27, 2006.
Sung-Yoon Lee	"A Korean Day of Infamy," *Weekly Standard*, January 23, 2006.
National Review	"Among the Darkest Pits of Cruelty and Horror in Today's World Are the Labor Camps of North Korea," April 24, 2006.
Bill Powell	"Running Out of the Darkness," *Time*, May 1, 2006.
David Scheffer & Grace Kang	"North Korea's Criminal Regime," *International Herald Tribune*, July 6, 2006.
South China Morning Post	"Democratic Beacon Shines in South Korea," January 10, 2007.
Jason Lee Steorts	"The Sham of 'Sunshine': South Korea's Policy Toward the North Does No Good," *National Review*, August 7, 2006.
Jennifer Veale	"Seoul Searching," *Foreign Policy*, January/February 2007.

For Further Discussion

Chapter 1

1. William Perry claims that coercion may be the only way to contain the North Korean nuclear threat. Gregory Elich, on the other hand, argues against coercive action, maintaining that coercive U.S. action is what led North Korea to test its nuclear capability in the first place. What kinds of evidence does each author use to support his claim? Which evidence do you find more persuasive? Explain, citing from the texts.

2. Brendan I. Koerner distinguishes between direct and indirect terrorist action. In your opinion, does this distinction make the author's claim that North Korea sponsors terrorism more or less persuasive? Does Ivan Eland make the same distinction to support his claim that North Korea does not sponsor terrorists? Does this impact the persuasiveness of his argument? Explain your answers, citing from the viewpoints.

3. Michael Richardson asserts that North Korean criminal activity finances the nation's nuclear weapons program. Kim Myong Chol denies such claims, arguing that criminal behavior on the part of the government would violate the principle of self-reliance that guides North Korean policy-making. Citing examples from the viewpoints, identify the rhetorical strategies each author uses to support his argument? Which strategy do you find most effective?

Chapter 2

1. Authors James Hackett, Bruce Bennett, and Nina Hachigian do not dispute that North Korea is a repressive, hos-

tile regime. Hackett, however, contends that negotiation is futile and advocates regime change. Bennett and Hachigian argue, on the other hand, that regime change could lead to a far worse crisis in the region. Which argument do you find more persuasive. Explain, citing from the viewpoints.

2. What commonalities in rhetoric, style, and type of evidence can be found among the viewpoints on each side of the North Korean policy debate in this chapter? Do any of the viewpoints suffer from logical fallacies? Explain, citing from the viewpoints.

3. Of the policies explored in this chapter, which do you think would be most effective? Citing from the viewpoint, explain your answer.

Chapter 3

1. Bruce Bennett cites the reunification of East and West Germany to support his claim that Korean unification will be costly for South Korea. Philip Bowring, however, maintains that Korean unification would more likely resemble the development of other once-struggling Asian communities to support his argument that the costs of Korean reunification have been exaggerated. Which comparison do you find more persuasive Explain, citing from the viewpoints.

2. Daniel Kennelly contends that the U.S. military should withdraw its troops from South Korea. Michael O'Hanlon claims, on the other hand, that abandoning its military command in South Korea would be dangerous for the United States. Citing examples from the viewpoints, what types of evidence does each author use to support his claim. Which do you find more persuasive and why?

3. *Hankyoreh*, a progressive South Korean newspaper, claims that South Korea should continue its engagement strategy with North Korea. Gregory Rodriguez, a U.S. think tank

scholar, claims that these failed policies are an embarrassment for the South Korean people. In what way do you think the affiliation of the authors influence their arguments? Do the authors' affiliations influence which argument you find more persuasive? Citing the texts, explain.

4. Of the policies explored in this chapter, which do you think would be most effective? Explain, citing from the viewpoints.

Chapter 4

1. Balbina Y. Hwang claims that some of the ideas that have emerged in the open forum of South Korea's evolving democracy, particularly policies toward North Korea, conflict with the views of its ally, the United States. In what way are these conflicts reflected in Nicholas Eberstadt's viewpoint, in which he argues that South Korea's democracy is threatened? Which viewpoint do you think best reflects the state of South Korean democracy? Citing from the texts, explain.

2. What rhetorical strategies does Jasper Becker use to support his claim that North Korea violates the human rights of its people? Cite examples of each rhetorical strategy from the text of his viewpoint.

3. Of the strategies proposed by John Feffer, the *Economist*, and Sung-Yoon Lee, which do you believe would most effectively promote human rights in North Korea? Explain your answer citing from the viewpoints.

Organizations to Contact

The editors have compiled the following list of organizations concerned with the issues debated in this book. The descriptions are derived from materials provided by the organizations. All have publications or information available for interested readers. The list was compiled on the date of publication of the present volume; the information provided here may change. Be aware that many organizations take several weeks or longer to respond to inquiries, so allow as much time as possible.

American Enterprise Institute (AEI)
1150 Seventeenth Street NW, Washington, DC   20036
Web site: www.aei.org

AEI is a conservative think tank based in Washington, DC. Its members support a strong and well-funded military and the containment of rogue nations such as North Korea, and those that support terrorism. AEI publishes the magazine *American Enterprise*. Other publications include "Facing a Nuclear North Korea" and "The Next Hotspot," which are available on its Web site.

American Foreign Policy Council (AFPC)
509 C Street NE, Washington, DC   20002
(202) 543-1006 • fax: (202) 543-1007
e-mail: afpc@afpc.org
Web site: www.afpc.org

Founded in 1982, AFPC is a nonprofit organization dedicated to bringing information to those who make or influence the foreign policy of the United States and to assisting world leaders with building democracies and market economies. AFPC publishes bulletins on foreign policy issues, including the *Missile Defense Briefing Report* and the *Asia Security Monitor*, which includes reports on North Korea. Recent issues of these publications are available on its Web site.

Amnesty International USA
Five Penn Plaza, New York, NY 10001
(212) 807-8400 • fax: (212) 627-1451
Web site: www.amnestyusa.org

Amnesty International works to ensure that governments do
not deny individuals their basic human rights as outlined in
the United Nations Universal Declaration of Human Rights. It
publishes numerous books, reports on individual countries,
and *Amnesty Now*, a quarterly magazine. Its Web site contains
recent news, reports, and a searchable database of archived
publications, including "Starved of Rights: Human Rights and
the Food Crisis in the Democratic People's Republic of Korea
(North Korea)."

Arms Control Association (ACA)
1313 L Street, NW, Suite 130, Washington, DC 20005
(202) 463-8270 • fax: (202) 463-8273
e-mail: aca@armscontrol.org
Web site: www.armscontrol.org

Founded in 1971, ACA promotes public understanding of and
support for effective arms control policies. It provides policy
makers, the press, and the public with information, analysis,
and commentary on arms control proposals, negotiations and
agreements, and related national security issues. ACA publishes the monthly *Arms Control Today*, recent issues of which
are available on its Web site. Archived articles available on its
Web site include "North Korea Increasing Weapons Capabilities" and "'Getting Serious' About North Korea."

Brookings Institution
1775 Massachusetts Ave. NW, Washington, DC 20036
(202) 797-6000 • fax: (202) 797-6004
e-mail: brookinfo@brook.edu
Web site: www.brook.edu

Founded in 1927, the institution conducts research and analyzes global events and their impact on the United States and
U.S. foreign policy. It publishes the quarterly *Brookings Review*

and numerous books and research papers on foreign policy. Numerous reports on foreign policy and North Korea are available on the institution's Web site, including *The New National Security Strategy and Preemption* and *A "Master" Plan to Deal with North Korea*.

Cato Institute

1000 Massachusetts Ave. NW, Washington, DC   20001-5403
(202) 842-0200 • fax: (202) 842-3490
Web site: www.cato.org

The institute is a libertarian public policy research foundation dedicated to peace and limited government intervention in foreign affairs. It publishes numerous reports and periodicals, including *Policy Analysis* and *Cato Policy Review*, both of which discuss U.S. policy in regional conflicts. CATO members publish analysis and commentary opposing the U.S. invasion of Iraq and the use of force against other nations, including North Korea, thought to support terrorism. Articles available on its Web site include, "Options for Dealing with North Korea," "North Korea Calls for Engagement, Not Isolation," and "Nuclear Neighbors Might Thwart N. Korea."

Center for Strategic and International Studies (CSIS)

1800 K St. NW, Washington, DC   20006
(202) 887-0200 • fax: (202) 775-3199
Web site: www.csis.org

CSIS is a public policy research institution that specializes in U.S. domestic and foreign policy, national security, and economic policy. The center analyzes world crises and recommends U.S. military and defense policies. Its publications include the journal *The Washington Quarterly* and the reports *Change and Challenge on the Korean Peninsula: Developments, Trends, and Issues* and *Combating Chemical, Biological, Radiological, and Nuclear Terrorism: A Comprehensive Strategy*.

Council on Foreign Relations (CFR)

58 E. Sixty-Eighth St., New York, NY   10021

(212) 434-9400 • fax: (212) 986-2984
Web site: www.cfr.org

The council specializes in foreign affairs and studies the international aspects of American political and economic policies and problems. Its journal *Foreign Affairs*, published five times a year, includes analyses of current conflicts around the world. Articles and commentary by CFR members are available on its Web site, including the report *A New National Security Strategy in an Age of Terrorists, Tyrants, and Weapons of Mass Destruction* and the *Backgrounder*, "North Korea: Parallel to Iraq?"

Federation of American Scientists (FAS)
1717 K St., NW, Suite 209, Washington, DC 20036
(202) 546-3300 • fax: (202) 675-1010
Web site: www.fas.org

FAS was formed in 1945 by atomic scientists from the Manhattan Project who felt that scientists had an ethical obligation to bring their knowledge and experience to bear on critical national decisions, especially pertaining to the technology they unleashed—the atomic bomb. Endorsed by 67 Nobel Laureates in chemistry, economics, medicine, and physics, FAS promotes humanitarian uses of science and technology. It publishes the seasonal *Public Interest Report*, recent issues of which are available on its Web site. Also on the Web site is a "Foreign Weapons Systems" link with articles on North Korea.

Heritage Foundation
214 Massachusetts Ave. NE, Washington, DC 20002-4999
(800) 544-4843 • fax: (202) 544-6979
e-mail: pubs@heritage.org
Web site: www.heritage.org

The foundation is a public policy research institute that advocates limited government and the free-market system. The foundation publishes the quarterly *Policy Review* as well as monographs, books, and papers supporting U.S. noninterventionism. Heritage publications on U.S. foreign policy include *Resolving the North Korean Nuclear Issue.*

Human Rights Watch

350 Fifth Ave., 34th Floor, New York, NY   10118-3299
(212) 290-4700
e-mail: hrwnyc@hrw.org
Web site: www.hrw.org

Founded in 1978, this nongovernmental organization conducts systematic investigations of human rights abuses in countries around the world including North Korea. It publishes many books and reports on specific countries and issues as well as annual reports, recent selections of which are available on its Web site.

Korea Society

950 Third Avenue, Eighth Floor, New York, NY   10022
(212) 759-7525
Web site: www.koreasociety.org

The Korea Society is a nonprofit organization that promotes better U.S.-Korea relations. The society arranges programs that facilitate discussion, exchanges, and research on topics of vital interest to both countries in the areas of public policy, business, education, intercultural relations, and the arts. It publishes annual reports and the *Korea Society Quarterly*, recent issues of which are available on its Web site.

Korean Central News Agency

e-mail: eng-info@kcna.co.jp
Web site: www.kcna.co.jp

Founded on December 5, 1946, the Korean Central News Agency is the official state-run news agency of the Democratic People's Republic of Korea, North Korea. The Web site publishes official government news releases to media in other countries with the stated goal of developing friendly and cooperative relations with foreign news agencies.

Nonproliferation Policy Education Center (NPEC)

1718 M St., NW, Suite 244, Washington, DC   20036

(202) 466-4406 • fax: (202) 659-5429
Web site: www.npec-web.org

NPEC supports a robust nonproliferation policy. The center's goal is to promote a deeper understanding of multiple perspectives on proliferation. NPEC publishes books and reports, some of which are available on its Web site. The center also publishes on its Web site previously published articles by NPEC staff, including "A Blink, a Nod, a Bomb" and "A World Provoked: Now How About We Do Something About Pyongyang?"

Nuclear Age Peace Foundation
1187 Coast Village Road, Suite 1, PMB 121
Santa Barbara, California   93108-2794
(805) 965-3443 • fax: (805) 568-466
Web site: www.wagingpeace.org

Founded in 1982, the Nuclear Age Peace Foundation, a nonprofit, nonpartisan international education and advocacy organization, initiates and supports worldwide efforts to abolish nuclear weapons, to strengthen international law and institutions, to use technology responsibly and sustainably, and to empower youth to create a more peaceful world. Its Web site, Wagingpeace.org, has a searchable database of news, editorials, and articles, including "North Korea's Nuclear Test: Turning Crisis into Opportunity" and "North Korean Nuclear Conflict Has Deep Roots."

Reason Foundation
3415 S. Sepulveda Blvd., Suite 400, Los Angeles, CA   90034
(310) 391-2245 • fax: (310) 391-4395
Web site: www.reason.org

The foundation promotes individual freedoms and free-market principles, and opposes U.S. interventionism in foreign affairs. Its publications include the monthly *Reason* magazine, recent issues of which are available at www.reason.com. The foundation Web site, linked to the Reason Public Policy Institute at www.rppi.org, publishes online versions of institute articles and reports, including "One Down, One to Go: Does the Nuke Deal with North Korea Make a U.S. Strike on Iran More Likely?"

U.S. Department of State
2201 C Street NW, Washington, DC   20520
Web site: www.state.gov

This State Department is a federal agency that advises the president on the formulation and execution of foreign policy. The Office of Counterterrorism publishes the annual report *Patterns of Global Terrorism*, which lists the nations that the United States has designated as state sponsors of terrorism; a list of United States' most wanted terrorists; and pages providing background information on every country in the world.

Bibliography of Books

Pyông-man An   *Elites and Political Power in South Korea.* Northampton, MA: Edward Elgar, 2003.

Tim Beal   *North Korea: The Struggle Against American Power.* Ann Arbor, MI: Pluto Press, 2005.

Jasper Becker   *Rogue State: The Continuing Threat of North Korea.* New York: Oxford University Press, 2005.

James Brady   *The Scariest Place in the World: A Marine Returns to North Korea.* New York: Thomas Dunne Books, 2005.

Peter Brookes   *A Devil's Triangle: Terrorism, Weapons of Mass Destruction, and Rogue States.* Lanham, MD: Rowman & Littlefield, 2005.

Gordon G. Chang   *Nuclear Showdown: North Korea Takes on the World.* New York: Random House, 2006.

Ivan Eland   *The Empire Has No Clothes: U.S. Foreign Policy Exposed.* Oakland, CA: Independent Institute, 2004.

John Feffer   *North Korea, South Korea: U.S. Policy at a Time of Crisis.* New York: Seven Stories, 2003.

Jack L. Goldsmith and Eric A. Posner   *Do International Norms Influence State Behavior?* New York: Oxford University Press, 2005.

Stephan Haggard and Marcus Noland — *Famine in North Korea: Markets, Aid, and Reform.* New York: Columbia University Press, 2007.

Linus Hagström and Marie Söderberg — *North Korea Policy: Japan and the Great Powers.* New York: Routledge, 2006.

Mark Edward Harris — *Inside North Korea.* San Francisco: Chronicle Books, 2007.

James Hoare — *North Korea in the 21st Century: An Interpretive Guide* Kent, UK: Global Oriental, 2005.

Ian Jeffries — *North Korea: A Guide to Economic and Political Developments.* New York: Routledge, 2006.

Young Whan Kihl and Hong Nack Kim, eds. — *North Korea: The Politics of Regime Survival.* Armonk, NY: M.E. Sharpe, 2006.

Hak-joon Kim — *North and South Korea: Internal Politics and External Relations Since 1988.* Mississauga, Ontario, Canada: Society for Korean and Related Studies, 2006.

Kyong Ju Kim — *The Development of Modern South Korea: State Formation, Capitalist Development and National Identity.* New York Routledge, 2006.

Andre Nikolaevich Lan'kov — *Crisis in North Korea: The Failure of De-Stalinization, 1956.* Honolulu: University of Hawaii Press, 2005.

Jan Lodal — *The Price of Dominance: The New Weapons of Mass Destruction and Their Challenge to American Leadership*. New York: Council of Foreign Relations, 2001.

James Irving Matray — *Korea Divided: The 38th Parallel and the Demilitarized Zone*. Philadelphia: Chelsea House, 2005.

Walter Russell Mead — *Power, Terror, Peace and War: America's Grand Strategy in a World at Risk*. New York: Knopf, 2004.

Robert M. Perito — *Where Is the Lone Ranger When We Need Him?: America's Search for a Postconflict Stability Force*. Washington, DC: United States Institute for Peace, 2004.

Sharon Richardson, ed. — *Perspectives on U.S. Policy Toward North Korea: Stalemate or Checkmate?* Lanham, MD: Lexington Books, 2006.

Jeffrey Richelson — *Spying on the Bomb: American Nuclear Intelligence, from Nazi Germany to Iran and North Korea*. New York: Norton, 2006.

Andrew Scobell — *Kim Jong Il and North Korea: The Leader and the System*. Carlisle Barracks, PA: Strategic Studies Institute, U.S. Army War College, 2006.

Key-young Son   *South Korean Engagement Policies and North Korea: Identities, Norms and the Sunshine Policy.* New York: Routledge, 2006.

William C.   *Rogue State: How a Nuclear North
Triplett   Korea Threatens America.* Washington, DC: Regnery, 2004.

William Walker   *Weapons of Mass Destruction and International Order.* New York: Oxford University Press, 2004.

Philip W. Yun   *North Korea: 2005 and Beyond.* Stan-
and Gi-Wook   ford, CA Brookings Institution Press,
Shin   2006.

Index